PRESERVING
MULTIGENERATIONAL
WEALTH

PRESERVING MULTIGENERATIONAL WEALTH

*How a Private Family Trust Company
Can Promote Family Harmony &
Positive Family Dynamics*

Cindy L. Steeb, MBA, JD

Copyright © 2023 by Cindy L. Steeb

All rights reserved. No part of this publication may be reproduced, stored in a retrieval system, stored in a database and/or published in any form or by any means, electronic, mechanical, photocopying, recording or otherwise, without the prior written permission of the author.

Information provided in this book is general in nature, is provided for informational purposes only, and should not be construed as financial, tax or legal advice. Making adjustments to a financial strategy or plan should only be undertaken after consulting with a professional. Particularly with estate planning or establishing a family trust company, working with a professional having specialized expertise in these areas is very important.

ISBN: 979-8-9895198-0-4

Published by CLS Publishing, LLC

I dedicate this book to my late parents, Clyde and Betty Steeb. They raised me to be bold and brave in life. It is their legacy of love and my desire to perpetuate our family farm that has driven my commitment to helping families preserve their family legacy—whatever that legacy may be—across generations. May they be looking down from heaven smiling at the daughter they raised.

Contents

	What Keeps You Up at Night?	ix
	My Story	xiii
	Goal of the Book	xvii
1	Getting on the Same Page	19
2	Family Businesses: Engines of the U.S. Economy	49
3	A Deeper Dive into FTCs	65
4	Benefits of FTCs	87
5	FTC Structures: An Overview	92
6	FTC Structures: Case Studies	113
7	Ongoing Operations	128
8	Parting Thoughts: Thinking of an FTC as a Solution	132
	Appendix	139

Acknowledgements

My sincere thanks to Gina G. Gurganus for her article in the Appendix highlighting the window of opportunity that exists until the end of 2025 when the lifetime exemption is set to sunset to a significantly lower amount. This makes estate planning a top priority for wealth creators and family-business owners—today!

I also want to thank Kelly Grupczynski Speck for the design of the book cover. Her creative talent and friendship are beyond measure! It's as if she knew what I wanted even when I didn't know!

Finally, a heartfelt thank you to David G. O'Neil of Story Trust for his editorial expertise and design of the book's interior pages. Without his patience, encouragement, and occasional scolding, this book would never have been finished! Truly a treasured part of this journey for me to publish a book!

What Keeps You Up at Night?

A Brief Survey

Family-business owners have a lot on their minds, not the least of which is maintaining the delicate balance between maintaining family harmony *and* running the business. For example, how do you manage the relationship dynamics among family members who are working in the business and those who are not working in the business? Which family members should you hire, and should you establish an Employment Policy with clear guidelines? Who in the family will be best suited to take over when you decide to step away from the business? Or will the next leader of the business be a non-family member? How will the family be able to maintain ownership of the business for generations to come? How do you ensure shareholders operate under the premise of "noses in but fingers out" so that they stay informed but don't interfere with the management of the family business? How do you educate and encourage shareholders to be good stewards of the family enterprise?

The phrase "shirtsleeves to shirtsleeves in three generations" reflects the often-repeated pattern where the first generation starts a business and works hard to build it up, the second generation manages to sustain it, and the third generation often sees a decline, resulting in the family returning to more modest "shirtsleeves" lifestyle, similar to their starting point two generations earlier. This phenomenon, which highlights the challenges of maintaining a successful business across multiple generations, is so universal that it can be found in various cultures and languages. In Japan the expression goes, "Rice paddies to rice paddies in three generations." The Scottish say, "The father buys, the son builds, the grandchild sells, and his son begs." And in Italy they express the same idea rather poetically: *Dalle stalle alle stelle e dalle stelle alle stalle*. It means, "From the stalls to the stars and from the stars back to the stalls."

The purpose of this book is to share a wealth management strategy option that can help families with wealth—including family-business owners—avoid "shirtsleeves to shirtsleeves" and address the associated challenges in a way that can create stability, peace of mind, and family harmony across the generations. Success in preserving family wealth often depends on proactive planning, effective governance structures, clear communication among family members, and a shared commitment to sustaining the family legacy. Implementing strategies using trusts, thoughtful estate planning, and family governance structures can help mitigate wealth erosion over time.

What Keeps You Up at Night?

To get started, please take a few moments to answer Yes or No to the following questions.

Question	Yes	No
If you died unexpectedly, would your business have to be sold to pay estate taxes?		
Have you projected the value of shareholder ownership into the future based on current growth to know if your estate, or other shareholder's estates, will owe estate tax at your death?		
If you answered "Yes" to the previous question, does the estate have the liquidity to pay the estate tax?		
Do you want to move assets out of your estate but want to continue to have a voice in shareholder decisions?		
Would your business be able to survive if you suddenly became disabled?		
Do you have a plan so that family-business ownership will not be fragmented in the future?		
Is the future ownership of your family business clearly defined and understood by shareholders?		
Have you determined how wealth—including family business shares—will pass through future generations in various family branches?		
Have you made a legacy plan that spells out the support you want to provide for your grandchildren, great-grandchildren, and so on?		
Have you resolved all family dynamics that might threaten familial harmony when the current family leader is no longer available?		

If you answered "No" to at least one of these, this book is for you. Answering "No" to these questions is more common than you think. Even large multi-generational families have missed dealing with important family shareholder issues. It's work. It takes time. It can be hard. It is important. Families that want to sustain the business across generations or stay together as a family across generations intentionally strive to keep family members informed and engaged. Are you a family-owned business or a business-owning family? Also, it is important to note that although this book focuses on transferring ownership of a family business asset, many of the concepts can also apply to families that have had a liquidity event or desire intergenerational wealth transfer.

My Story

THE REASON I do estate planning is because of what happened to my family.

In 1997, my dad died suddenly in an accident when his bulldozer flipped over on him. Two months later, my mom, a non-smoker, was diagnosed with terminal lung cancer.

I moved home to take care of Mom, leaving my career in sales and marketing at a subsidiary of United Airlines. I moved from Chicago to live with her at our family farm in northern Ohio. Given my mom's health condition, I helped her extensively in her role as executor of my dad's estate.

My parents had not done any estate planning, other than executing a Will back in 1965. They purchased their farm in 1962 and by the time Dad died, the value of the land had appreciated tremendously. Like so many in similar circumstances, my family was facing an estate tax bill when my mom would pass away, largely based on an illiquid asset—our farm. The only way we could pay the tax would be to sell our family home and/or the farm.

Unbeknownst to them, my parents' lack of planning had put our family legacy in jeopardy. It soon became obvious that they also were not working with an attorney with the proper expertise in estate planning. We found a new attorney who focused solely on estate planning, and she helped us address issues with my dad's estate along with rushing to put together a workable estate plan for my mom. The whole process was overwhelming. Mom was reeling from Dad's death—we were all grieving the sudden loss of a husband and dad. It was not a good time, to say the least, to be dealing with complex legal and financial issues.

Thankfully, my mom went into remission. Even so, when pushed, her doctors admitted that her life expectancy wasn't nearly as long as we'd hoped. I decided I wanted to stay in Ohio and not return to Chicago. My mom was my best friend, and I wanted to spend as much time with her as I could.

After seeing what my mother endured trying to fix the estate plans, I decided to switch careers and go to law school to study estate planning. I had a very specific goal in mind: I wanted to help other families NOT go through what my family went through. Cleveland State offered me a full-tuition scholarship. If that wasn't God telling me what I was supposed to be doing, I don't know what is.

After graduating, I started at a firm in their estate planning group. Very soon, though, they wanted me doing probate litigation because of my sales background. The rationale was that I would make a great litigator with a history of thinking on my feet and doing presentations in my sales career. Soon, I was in court dealing with families that were disputing some aspect of a loved one's estate plan. I hated it.

After one very contentious family meeting—seven adult children fighting over a very modest estate—I told the partner I was with, "They don't need attorneys, they need family therapy, and the only people that are going to win here are the attorneys." She seemed heartened to focus on the size of the legal fees that would mean. My heart sank.

I went to my car and told myself, "I can't do this. I won't do this." I will not make a living participating in events that tear families apart. Then and there I decided I needed a different way to practice law. That opportunity came when a recruiter reached out about a job in a family office. A perfect fit. Family offices are designed to help families and keep them together across generations. Now my focus and purpose are to harmonize families. I look at estate planning as a gift you leave your family—a Family Trust Company is just the "bow on top"!

I probably could have made a whole lot more money in probate litigation, but it doesn't matter. I wasn't interested. I really wanted to do something positive and work to make the world a better place for me having been here.

Goal of the Book

My goal in writing this book is to explore using trusts with a Family Trust Company as trustee to increase the chances of a business continuing beyond the shirtsleeves to shirtsleeves in three generations dilemma. Transferring shares of a family business into a trust may help hold the business together. It does this by consolidating shareholder decisions into a smaller group of family members (or trusted advisors) as the size of the family continues to expand generation after generation while allowing the possibility of passing the economic benefit of the family business along to family members—now and into the future. A Family Trust Company, by its structure, has family members working together across generations, which can build the one thing that helps keep families together—trust!

I will explore estate planning utilizing trusts, coupled with creating a Family Trust Company to serve as trustee of the family trusts. The question becomes how can an estate plan that facilitates shareholder transition be structured to provide opportunities to keep the family together doing well? I had a client who always told me, "When the family is doing well, the business can do well, and when the business is doing well, the family can do well." It's impossible to decouple the family from the business and vice versa. It's like being on a boat and trying to have everyone rowing at the same pace and in the same direction. As with a team of rowers, what one person does impacts the rest of the crew. How can family members continue to row in the same direction? Planning, or lack of planning, by one family member may significantly impact other family members who are in the same boat—positively or negatively.

Like most things in life, you get out of something what you put into it. This book highlights the great flexibility provided under a Family Trust Company showcasing the Board and various committees that can support a family in addition to the family business. Although a Family Trust Company can provide the platform for great transparency and the opportunity for family members to work together, family members still need to put in the time and effort to make a Family Trust Company successful. The roadmap can be laid out, but the cars still need drivers.

CHAPTER 1

Getting on the Same Page

Before diving headlong into the intricacies and practicalities of Family Trust Companies (FTCs), I'd like to step back for a moment and review a few key estate-planning concepts that are essential to understanding the need that FTCs fill. If you are very familiar with these terms, feel free to skip ahead or skim just to refresh your memory.

We will start with the fundamental elements of revocable and irrevocable trusts and explore the crucial roles of grantors, beneficiaries, and trustees. Building from there, we'll review the most common trustee options and explore their pros and cons. To top it off, we'll examine the intricate dance between trustees and beneficiaries, exploring how FTCs can transform a relationship of dependence and suspicion into one that is harmonious with more transparency while building a lasting legacy.

Trusts Basics

You are probably aware that there are many kinds of trusts—some revocable and some irrevocable—serving many functions. For our purposes, I would like to briefly explain how trusts work in the context of transferring ownership of a family-owned business to future generations.

Let's start with some definitions:

Grantor

The **grantor**, also known as the settlor or trustor, is the person who creates the trust. They transfer ownership of assets, such as shares in a family business, into the trust. The grantor defines the trust's terms, including how the assets are to be managed and distributed.

Beneficiary

In general, a **beneficiary** is an individual, group, or entity designated to receive the benefits or assets from a trust. They are entitled to various rights, which may include receiving distributions and potentially having a say in certain decisions, depending on the terms of the trust. They have a beneficial interest in the assets in the trust rather than direct ownership—the assets in the trust aren't "theirs." For example, a beneficiary could receive distributions of the dividends declared by the family business which went to the trust as a shareholder of the family business. However, instead of directly receiving the dividends, the decision to distribute the dividend to the beneficiary is made by the trustee (read on for more on the trustee's role).

Trustees

The **trustee** is a person or entity responsible for managing the assets held in the trust on behalf of the beneficiaries. Trustees have a fiduciary duty to act in the best interests of the beneficiaries and follow the grantor's intention as expressed through the trust's terms. The role of the trustee is particularly important when the trust holds ownership of a family business since the trustee makes or votes on shareholder decisions related to the shares of the family business in the trust.

Adding to the complexity, there are various types of trustees:

- A **corporate trustee** is typically a financial institution, bank, or institutional trust company. They have specialized knowledge and experience in trust administration, investments, and financial management. Corporate trustees offer professionalism and consistency, but may be perceived as less personal with rigid policies and procedures. A corporate trustee may also be hesitant to hold a concentrated asset such as a family business as the primary asset in a trust which could create pressure to diversify this investment. Given a corporate trustee's profit motive, they can also be expensive. In recent years, bank mergers and acquisitions have led to a rapid turnover in personnel leaving a beneficiary making requests of and working with a stranger.

- An **individual trustee** is a person chosen by the grantor to oversee the trust. This could be a family member, a trusted friend, or an advisor. Individual trustees can be cost effective and provide a personal touch but may lack the expertise or resources of a corporate trustee. Individuals also don't live forever, so thinking about who will be the trustee for grandchildren and great-grandchildren can be challenging. Whatever knowledge of the family an individual trustee may have it can be lost and become unavailable for the benefit of future generations. If naming a family member as trustee, delicate and complicated relationship dynamics can be created including if a beneficiary asks for a distribution from the trust—what if the distribution is needed for a very private reason such as infertility medical expenses? What if the individual trustee refuses to make a distribution that the beneficiary was counting on? Sadly, having an individual trustee that is a family member can make for a strained Thanksgiving dinner!

- A **family trust company**, also called a private trust company in some states, is a family-owned and -controlled entity whose sole purpose is the management of assets for the benefit of a single-family lineage. FTCs are authorized by state statute and not all states have created these laws. In those states with the proper statutes, an FTC does provide customized and centralized control over family trusts when the FTC is named as trustee for these trusts. Family trusts are those set up by family members for the benefit of family members. An FTC empowers families to create and control a highly personalized and flexible wealth strategy, ensuring the preservation, strategic growth, and responsible transfer of assets across generations. All this is possible because the FTC is the trustee, with a board and committees comprised of family members and trusted advisors making the various decisions required of a trustee—decisions don't get more personalized than this! An FTC can be pivotal for a family business—when a grantor places shares of the family business in a trust, family members, as part of the FTC structure, can continue to make shareholder decisions related to the family business.

Below is a table detailing some of the characteristics of each trustee option:

Traditional Corporate	Individual	Family Trust Company
• Regulated • Professional • Rigid Policies • Conservative • Changing Personnel • Expensive • Accountable • Impersonal	• Sensitive and Knowledgeable about Family • Flexible/Subjective (Saying "no" is difficult.) • Private • Not Expensive • Not Permanent • Individual Fiduciary Liability • Susceptible to Family Dynamics	• Confidential • Trustee is Permanent • Institutionalizes the Personal, Business, and Investment Matters for a Family • Personalized Service • Liability Protection • Flexibility in Managing Concentrated Financial Positions • Infused with Family Values

Historically, a corporate trustee was the only option if you wanted a permanent trustee for long-term trusts. Although corporate trustees are aware of the legal requirements to act as trustee, there are also downsides to a corporate trustee given that mergers in the banking industry can lead to ever-changing personnel. New trust officers start working with family members without a true understanding of the family's business and value system. As expected, a corporate trustee will be litigation averse, so they may approach investments and distributions very conservatively—or require the portfolio be invested in the corporate trustee's products. Even with a waiver of the duty to diversify included in the trust documents, corporate trustees can remain hesitant about holding a concentrated asset like a family business thus wanting to sell all, or portions, of the family business ownership in the trust. In addition, to properly manage the trust assets, the corporate trustee, as part of their oversight of the assets held in the trust, will have access to the family business' financials and other operational details. Potentially, an outside corporate trustee may also lack patience to remain invested in the family business should the family business hit upon rough times. Lastly, since corporate trustees operate under a profit motive they are likely the most expensive option for trusteeship.

Many families have preferred to utilize an individual trustee, someone who knows the family's values and role of the family business for the family—not to mention the familiarity with family dynamics. Typically, the individual trustee is from a separate family branch of the grantor. For example, an uncle would serve as trustee of his niece's or nephew's trust. Another option for an individual trustee is a trusted advisor of the grantor. Beyond the obvious disadvantage that an individual doesn't live forever, both of these approaches come with challenges. Individuals aren't always aware of the legal requirements for being a trustee, nor do they understand tax implications of different decisions, which can lead to some unexpected tax consequences. An individual can let personal bias determine if a distribution is appropriate or not. A trusted advisor of the grantor may not know, or understand, the aspirations of the grantor's child—the beneficiary. The grantor's child may not be comfortable engaging with a parent's advisor to appropriately share information. Family relationships can become strained when the beneficiary disagrees with decisions made by the trustee, particularly related to investments or distributions. For the individual trustee, they may not understand the individual fiduciary liability they are taking on, but are rather doing a favor for the grantor. None of this sets up the trustee/beneficiary relationship to create positive dynamics that benefit the beneficiary and the family business (if some ownership of the family business is in the trust).

Forming an FTC to serve as the trustee for family trusts serves to institutionalize the personal, business, and investment matters for a family while also preserving and instilling family values in those matters. An FTC is a permanent trustee solution as it is a company set up to continue in perpetuity. Since the FTC is owned and controlled by family, its board, officers and committee members intimately understand the importance of the family business to the family members (the trust beneficiaries). This lessens the concern of holding a concentrated position with more tolerance for the potential ebbs and flows of the return from a family business. Additionally, the FTC can offer very personalized service tailored for the needs of the family but with the professional consistency of documented policies and procedures. Those serving on the Board and Committees of the FTC understand the role of the family business, understand sensitive family dynamics and understand (supported by the proper advisors) the fiduciary responsibilities of a trustee. Therefore, the FTC creates a combination of the positives of a corporate trustee and an individual trustee in one entity!

Liability protection cannot be underestimated. As mentioned above, individuals serving as trustee have personal fiduciary liability. An FTC also has fiduciary liability, but the policies and procedures developed when setting up an FTC offer liability protection in standardizing decision making related to the trusts as well as ensuring state law trust requirements are followed. In analyzing decisions, the business judgement rule is applied when evaluating whether the FTC's policies—evidenced by robust documentation—have been followed. When considering the trustee options, an FTC can offer the best characteristics of an individual trustee with the longevity and structure of a corporate trustee—the best of both worlds!

As you can imagine, the grantor/trustee/beneficiary relationships can be difficult to navigate due to the possibility of different objectives in each role. Strengthening these relationships and providing transparency as to trust terms and how decisions are made can go a long way in making the trustee/beneficiary relationship a positive experience. When family trusts are overseen by different, separate trustees, beneficiaries frequently receive different, and sometimes conflicting, information leading to confusion and distrust. Family members talk to each other and compare notes in an effort to gather more information. An FTC can be structured to encourage communication, education and even mentorship amongst these relationships leading to more trust among the family and the family business. With family members involved in the FTC through seats on the Board and Committees, a focus on family values can be maintained while family members come to understand the trustee/beneficiary dynamic to become better stewards of the family wealth.

Within the context of an FTC, beneficiaries would be those family members for whom the trust services are established to manage and safeguard assets for their benefit since FTCs only serve family members. In the context of an FTC, family members are defined beyond the grantor's lineal descendants. For example, under Ohio law, an FTC can also serve spouses, former spouses, stepchildren, and adopted children of the grantor—plus trusts set up for their benefit. As touched on above, if family-business ownership is placed in the trust, the beneficiaries now have **beneficial ownership** of the family business versus direct ownership. These beneficial owners don't actually own these shares in the business—the trust owns the shares. This shift from prior generations in how the family business ownership is structured—critical in many families to minimize estate taxes at the elder generation passing—requires education and understanding of the shift in how shareholder decisions must be made. Thus, through succeeding generations as shareholders create trusts to minimize estate taxes, more and more family members will not directly own a family business, but rather the trusts will become the owners of the family business. This makes the role of the trustee ever increasing in importance.

"May I have more, please?"

While the benefits of establishing trusts for family members are many, some research has shown that there are many unintended consequences baked into the traditional trustee/beneficiary relationship. One study asked trust beneficiaries if being a beneficiary was more a burden or a blessing. Eighty percent of the group said "burden."[1] Probably the opposite of what you would expect—or desire for your family.

One main reason for this surprising result is the potentially troublesome dynamic between the beneficiary and the trustee. I call it the "May I Have a Penny?" Syndrome. The classic scenario is that the beneficiary goes to the trustee and asks for a discretionary distribution—perhaps to pursue an advanced degree or start a new business. Despite sincere intentions by the beneficiary to use the funds wisely, the trustee, for whatever reason, says, "No." Even the requirement to "ask" for money can be awkward—particularly for adult beneficiaries. This dynamic of dependency can be the cause of much frustration and hurt for both the beneficiary and the trustee. Beneficiaries have expressed continuing to feel like a child well into adulthood given the complicated relationship with a trustee. In addition, beneficiaries can be frustrated by the lack of involvement in decisions related to the assets held in the trusts, coupled with the all-too-common lack of information shared with the beneficiary regarding the assets in a trust.

This potentially adversarial relationship between trustee and beneficiary can be handled in a much healthier way in the context of an FTC. All FTCs, as I'll explain in more detail later, have Discretionary Distributions Committees (DDCs) that have policies and procedures so members of the DDC manage distribution requests, typically with a level of transparency into how the process works and decisions are made. Rather than have requests fall on the shoulders of one individual trustee (often a family member or close friend/trusted advisor of the grantor) or the faceless bureaucracy of a corporate trustee, the decisions by the FTC can create more transparency and take into account intimate knowledge of the life circumstances of each beneficiary as well as the family's vision and values. All beneficiaries have the same experience as well working with one trustee—the FTC. It eliminates the discrepancy of beneficiaries getting different information from different trustees, which creates an experience akin to "telephone" played as child when each person gets a little correct information but no one understands the entire story. In the best circumstances, DDC members strive to become mentors to the beneficiaries—perhaps a sounding board to the beneficiary for a distribution requested to start a business or seek higher education. For example, a DDC can ask a beneficiary for a business plan as part of such a request then provide feedback on the business plan. With a highly functioning DDC, both the beneficiary and the DDC take responsibility for making the trustee/beneficiary relationship a positive experience.

Thoughtful Estate Planning & The Continuum of Trust Planning

Think of the various legal mechanisms and strategies in trust planning as falling along a continuum, each offering a unique blend of control and permanence to effectively manage your assets and legacy. It starts with revocable planning tools, granting you control throughout your lifetime and allowing you to direct their disposition beyond your passing. Next comes irrevocable planning structures, each carefully crafted to fulfill specific objectives, such as mitigating estate taxes or safeguarding a family business or wealth for generations to come. Among these irrevocable strategies is the Dynasty Trust, a powerful vehicle for preserving not only your ownership in various assets but also the enduring prosperity of your family as assets placed in a Dynasty Trust are out of not only the grantor's estate, but all future generations' estates as well. As you can imagine, the irrevocable trust planning requires more thoughtful consideration due to the permanency of the trust terms. Continue reading for more insight into the significance and implications of Dynasty Trusts and how they fit within the broader spectrum of estate planning. Let's explore each level of planning in greater detail.

Revocable Planning

There are three documents that are effective solely during your lifetime: 1) Durable Power of Attorney, 2) Health Care Power of Attorney and 3) Living Will (in some states the Health Care Power of Attorney and the Living Will are combined and referred to as Health Care Directives). Let's explore each one of these documents as they are important to a comprehensive estate plan even if they don't directly impact the transfer of assets to the next generation.

A **Durable Power of Attorney** (POA) grants a trusted individual, often called an attorney-in-fact or agent, the authority to make important financial decisions on your behalf if you ever become incapacitated. This document ensures the seamless management of your affairs, such as paying bills, managing investments, and handling real estate transactions. Even access to information about utilities can be blocked without an agent being given this authority under a POA. If ownership in the family business is held in an individual name, the attorney-in-fact will be the person who has the authority to make shareholder decisions based on your ownership. A POA is a powerful document in that the attorney-in-fact "steps into your shoes" and has access to your detailed financial matters. It's important to note that this authority doesn't extend to assets held in a trust, as the trustee oversees all the assets in the trust. At your passing, this document is no longer effective and the attorney-in-fact ceases to have any authority over your assets.

For example, consider a scenario where you were involved in a severe accident rendering you unconscious and unable to attend to your financial responsibilities. In this situation, your appointed agent steps in to safeguard your interests and ensure your financial matters remain in order, preventing potential chaos and hardship for your loved ones. The appointed agent could vote any shares of the family business as included in your financial responsibilities absent a separate agreement.

Similar to a Durable Power of Attorney, but tailored to healthcare decisions, a **Health Care Power of Attorney** designates a healthcare proxy to make crucial medical choices when you're unable to communicate your wishes. This includes decisions regarding surgeries and treatments. Imagine a scenario where you are in a coma due to a sudden illness. Your healthcare agent, guided by any pre-stated preferences, collaborates with medical professionals to make informed decisions on your behalf, ensuring that your medical care aligns with your wishes.

A **Living Will** is another essential component of revocable planning. This document allows you to outline your specific medical treatment preferences for life-sustaining treatment in case you're unable to communicate them directly, but are not expected to survive your injuries or illness. For instance, you can specify whether you wish to receive specific medical measures, such as artificial respiration or tube feeding, under certain circumstances. By providing clear directives, you relieve your family members of the emotional burden of making these challenging decisions on your behalf during already stressful times.

Revocable Planning that Becomes Irrevocable Upon Your Death

A **Last Will and Testament**, commonly known as a Will, articulates your wishes regarding the distribution of your assets after your passing. It enables you to name beneficiaries, specify bequests, and appoint an executor to oversee the distribution of your assets based on your wishes. For example, your Will might stipulate that your home goes to your spouse, a portion of your savings to your grandchildren, and charitable donations to your favorite causes. Importantly, a Will is a revocable instrument during your lifetime, allowing you to make changes as circumstances evolve. It is imperative to note that assets passing using a Will are distributed to a beneficiary upon them reaching the age of majority (the age varies by state but is commonly 18 years old). Depending upon the amount and type of assets, an eighteen year old may not have the wisdom to properly manage the inheritance. Also, assets passing using only a Will are subject to probate in most states. Probate is court oversight of your estate including the distribution of your assets. In many states, the probate process is public record so, for example, family-business ownership—including the value of the family business—may be able to be reviewed by the general public—including your competitors thus providing them with confidential information which ultimately may be disadvantageous to the family business. To avoid the probate process, assets may be placed in a Revocable Trust before passing as assets in revocable trusts are not part of your probate estate.

A **Revocable Trust**, sometimes referred to as a Living Trust, is a versatile estate planning tool that can simplify the management and distribution of your assets. While you're alive and well, you maintain full control over the trust, including the ability to amend or revoke it at any time. This flexibility is especially beneficial if you anticipate changes in your financial situation or family dynamics—for example, you may want to utilize these assets during your lifetime to fund your lifestyle. Also, after your passing, the assets in the trust may be distributed to a beneficiary outright over a longer period of time (or held in trust across generations) —unlike the Will which assets are distributed when a minor reaches the age of majority. Upon your death, a revocable trust becomes irrevocable, meaning it cannot be altered by anyone including your spouse or your children. As mentioned above, a revocable trust is particularly useful in avoiding the probate process, ensuring a more efficient and private distribution of your estate. This is particularly important for family-business ownership to ensure the confidentiality of the value company as well as the succeeding ownership.

Irrevocable Planning

An irrevocable trust requires the grantor to relinquish "dominion and control" over the trust assets upon placing the assets into the trust. The grantor typically gives up this control for estate tax reasons, gift reasons, privacy reasons, or protection from creditors. The assets placed into an irrevocable trust are no longer the grantor's property. An irrevocable trust is generally unchangeable once established, with some exceptions to update administrative terms. One way to think about assets placed in an irrevocable trust is legacy planning—assets that you want to ensure are passed to future generations, but that you aren't planning on relying on to fund your lifestyle during your lifetime.

If properly structured, the assets in an irrevocable trust are not only out of the grantor's estate, but they can be out of the reach of a beneficiary's creditors when the assets remain in the trust. This can be attractive if a beneficiary has embarked on a career subject to a high likelihood of litigation, such as a doctor. In addition, an estranged spouse in a domestic dispute is considered a creditor so assets held in an irrevocable trust can be out of consideration in a property division. Interestingly, in recent years, there has been a rise in using irrevocable trust planning in lieu of pre-nuptial agreements. More frequently, the rising generation is increasingly unwilling to execute a pre-nuptial agreement even if it is designed to protect a family business. However, an irrevocable trust can provide similar protections if properly drafted.

Some irrevocable trusts are set up for a specific purpose. Two common planning approaches are for an irrevocable trust to own a life insurance policy or to be used to make annual exclusion gifts. Let's explore each further.

An **Irrevocable Life Insurance Trust**, commonly referred to as an ILIT, is a specialized trust designed to hold life insurance policies. Once established, the terms and provisions of the ILIT cannot be changed or revoked by the grantor. The primary objective of an ILIT is to ensure proceeds of a life insurance policy are not includable in the estate of the insured person. In practical terms, the ILIT owns a life insurance policy on a particular individual—frequently the family-business owner holding substantial ownership in the company. This means the ILIT becomes the policyholder and beneficiary of the insurance coverage. When the insured person passes away, the insurance proceeds are paid into the trust for the benefit of the beneficiaries, who are frequently the grantor's spouse and/or lineal descendants. Since the policy is no longer part of the insured person's estate, its proceeds are not subject to estate taxes. This strategy ensures that the intended beneficiaries receive the insurance payout without the burden of significant estate tax liabilities. Although beyond the scope of this book, there are many strategies utilizing trusts and insurance in the safeguarding of a family business to future generations.

An **Annual Exclusion Gifting Trust** serves as a tool for gifting money or assets to loved ones in a tax-efficient manner while avoiding having a minor receive the assets upon turning the age of majority. Similar to the ILIT, this trust is irrevocable, meaning that once assets are placed into the trust, they cannot be reclaimed by the grantor.

The annual gift tax exclusion allows individuals to give a certain amount of money or assets (e.g., family business-ownership) each year to another person without triggering gift tax obligations. The annual exclusion amount is set by the IRS each year and indexes for inflation over time. (In 2023, the annual exclusion amount is $17,000 per individual, which means that a couple can gift up to $34,000 each year to anyone without gift taxes.) By utilizing an Annual Exclusion Gifting Trust, the grantor can make gifts up to this exclusion amount to their beneficiaries without gift taxes, but the assets in the trust are overseen by a trustee instead of directly in the hands of the beneficiary.

The key advantage of this trust is that it allows the grantor to pass on wealth while having a trustee oversee the assets in the trust. This is particularly helpful when gifting to minor beneficiaries because when assets are gifted to a minor outright, the minor receives the assets upon attaining the age of majority which varies by state, but is typically in the range of 18 years old to 25 years old. This may not be desired—particularly for ownership in a family business. It also offers a structured approach to gifting over time if annual exclusion gifts are made each year, thus helping to minimize the estate taxes for the grantor. Another benefit is consolidating the control of assets held in each trust by naming the same trustee for each of the annual exclusion gifting trusts. This is particularly helpful when transitioning ownership in a family business, but wanting to minimize the increasing number of individuals as shareholders. While the assets placed in this trust are no longer under the direct control of the grantor, they provide a means to support loved ones while minimizing the impact of gift and estate taxes plus consolidating the decision making for assets in trusts. This is particularly true if an FTC is named trustee of multiple Annual Exclusion Gifting Trusts established for various family members. For example, a family-business owner can establish an Annual Exclusion Gifting Trust for each of his grandchildren then transfer some ownership each year. With the FTC at the helm as the Trustee, shareholder decisions remain firmly within the purview of the family.

Dynasty Trusts

The next kind of irrevocable trust is frequently called a Dynasty Trust, but sometimes called a Perpetuity Trust or Multigenerational Trust. Assets placed in a Dynasty Trust are legacy assets—assets you typically no longer need to fund your lifestyle but you want to benefit your family across generations such as a family business remaining owned by family. It is designed to pass wealth through succeeding generations without being depleted by estate taxes as assets placed in a Dynasty Trust are outside of the grantor's taxable estate but also outside the beneficiaries' taxable estates across generations. Even the appreciation on the assets placed in the Dynasty Trust are not subject to estate taxes thus making it a good planning technique for a growing family business that is appreciating in value—sometimes referred to as freezing the asset. In 2023, a grantor can pass $12.92 million of assets to future generations using a Dynasty Trust without paying gift taxes (see the Appendix for an important potential reduction in this amount at the end of 2025 making planning very time sensitive). Also, a Dynasty Trust is typically set up to have no termination date to fully take advantage of passing assets across generations without incurring estate taxes. The assets continue to be held for the benefit of the grantor's lineal descendants essentially "forever." Beneficiaries may have beneficial enjoyment of the assets in the trust if discretionary distributions are made by the trustee, but they don't have direct ownership while the assets are in the trust. This makes selecting the trustee of a Dynasty Trust a crucial decision as the trustee controls the assets in the trust for the benefit of the beneficiaries across time.

A specific type of Dynasty Trust is a spousal lifetime access trust—commonly called a SLAT. A SLAT is an irrevocable trust that is held for the primary benefit of the grantor's spouse, but it may also include other family members as beneficiaries. This is a technique frequently used when a couple isn't certain if they will need access to trust assets in the future for unknown expenses or to maintain their lifestyle. Although the grantor still gives up dominion and control of assets placed in a SLAT—so the assets and their appreciation are out of the grantor's taxable estate with the spouse as the beneficiary—the trustee may make distributions to the spouse beneficiary which provides a flow of assets back into the household. However, there is a caution to setting up a SLAT in the event of death of the spouse beneficiary or a divorce. The grantor's household access would end in either event. Care must also be taken in drafting a SLAT to terminate the spouse as a beneficiary if the grantor and beneficiary divorce. Another important consideration is that the grantor retains responsibility for any income taxes related to assets held in a SLAT so planning to have liquidity to cover the taxes is important. However, this planning approach has continued to gain in popularity.

Dynasty Trusts are a beneficial shareholder transition method in situations when family members may want to stay connected to the family legacy as shareholders accruing the company's economic benefit (i.e., dividends), but do not want to be involved in the day-to-day operations of the family business. Understanding if family members consider ownership in the family business as a legacy asset versus a financial asset can be helpful in shareholder transition planning. Although there is a sliding scale between a legacy asset and a financial asset, many family members, even by the third generation, can consider the family business a legacy asset that is part of the family heritage—they want to keep ownership in the business because it's something their grandfather started. Pride, connection, family—just some of the words that I've heard used to describe the importance of a legacy asset. On the other hand, a financial asset is viewed solely based on the return on investment in the asset. Families that work to keep the stories alive about the hard work and dedication it took to build the family business more frequently have shareholders who tend to view the family business as a legacy asset. Sometimes referred to as "family glue" activities, bringing the family together for various events can be important to keeping family members viewing the family business as a legacy asset with the associated desire to maintain ownership—even if their ownership is through beneficial ownership of shares held for their benefit in a trust. I'll highlight later how an FTC can be designed to support family glue activities. Passing a legacy asset to future generations using a Dynasty Trust is a very effective shareholder transition plan.

In addition, the formation of a Dynasty Trust can reduce redemption pressure on a company in the event a shareholder dies with an estate tax bill related to illiquid family business ownership and the estate's executor turns to the company to provide liquidity to pay the estate taxes. There are many examples of family businesses that had to be sold due to lack of estate planning and the associated estate tax bill. Even if the business doesn't have to be sold, the associated estate tax liability can significantly impact the company's ability to innovate and grow. An unexpected passing or multiple shareholders' deaths close in time, could put a company in jeopardy without advance planning.

So, placing shares in a Dynasty Trust outside the purview of estate taxes can be imperative for the multigenerational continuation of a family business. Now, a significant consideration is who oversees the shares of the family business placed in the trust. A grantor may know who could serve as the current trustee, but who will be the future trustees given the forever nature of a Dynasty Trust? Grantors may have family members and/or advisors they are comfortable with serving today, but who will serve as trustee for family members in the future? Who will vote the family business shares when the grandchildren and great-grandchildren are the beneficial owners of the company? Who will help guide future generations in understanding what it means to be a good steward of the family business? Many times these questions weigh so heavily on the family business-owner that he or she just stops shareholder transition planning. But shareholder transition planning remains important to ensure the continuation of the business.

Traditionally, this important trustee choice consisted of either a corporate trustee or an individual (frequently a family member). Having an FTC serve as trustee may encompass positive characteristics of a corporate trustee and individual trustee.

Family Case: Five G2 Siblings

Consider the family with five G2 siblings. Each of the siblings owned shares of the family business and wanted to set up Dynasty Trusts to pass the shares of the company to future generations. They quickly realized that each G2 sibling could select a different trustee. Each trustee could have a different perspective on the desired performance of the family business, have varying knowledge about the company and/or family, and have a different perspective on their willingness to hold a concentrated asset in the trust. The impact of separate trustees could result in additional distractions to management at the family business as the different trustees reach out requesting information or questioning management decisions. Instead, the family established an FTC with a Board consisting of Family Branch Representatives as well as two independent, trusted advisors. The trusted advisors also served on various committees of the FTC. As a shareholder of the family business, the FTC Board votes on the Directors on the Board of the family-owned business as well as oversees the committees responsible for directing the investing of any liquidity in the trusts, distributing assets from the trusts, and providing educational programming to the beneficiaries of the trusts—the family members. Therefore, through establishing an FTC to serve as trustee of the family's Dynasty Trusts, the family members remain the dominant voice in guiding the family and the family business across generations.

Business Succession Planning vs Shareholder Transition Planning

At this stage, it would be useful to make an important distinction between Business Succession Planning (BSP) and Shareholder Transition Planning (STP)—particularly since the term is used above in describing a Dynasty Trust. They seem similar and can often overlap, but clearly understanding the difference between the two is necessary to appreciating the solutions to the sleepless nights I am describing.

Business Succession Planning is a comprehensive strategy aimed at ensuring the smooth changeover of leadership and management within a business. That can mean passing the leadership torch from one generation of the family to the next, but not always, especially if there is no one in the family prepared to lead the enterprise. It often involves executing a strategy that allows business owners to exit the business on their terms and conditions while remaining confident that the family business will continue to be managed successfully through future generations.

As with finding leaders for any organization, BSP involves identifying and preparing individuals to take on key roles and responsibilities, ensuring the continuity of operations, decision-making, and overall organizational stability. And it can encompass leadership positions at various levels within a company. Its goal is to minimize disruptions and maintain the company's momentum during leadership changes. Estate planning doesn't impact BSP—those decisions remain with the management of the business which can include both family members and non-family members.

Questions related to BSP include:

- Would your business be able to survive if you were disabled? If so, for how long?
- Is there a second-in-command (family or non-family) whom you are mentoring, or have plans to develop?
- What is your timeline for being less active in the business, departing on a permanent basis, or changing ownership or control?
- If you have family members in your business, what objective criteria do you use to evaluate your family members' strengths, weakness, skills, and talents in evaluation of their potential as possible successors? Do they each have a mentor or other support in developing leadership skills and expertise to contribute to the family business?

- Do the family shareholders understand and support the leadership succession plan?

Shareholder Transition Planning, on the other hand, focuses specifically on the transfer of ownership of a business, usually from one generation to the next so it's very focused on the family. STP considers the required actions and estate planning methods needed to transition ownership and control of a family business intergenerationally. The aim is to ensure that ownership transfers align with the family's values and vision, minimize potential conflicts, and maintain the stability of the ownership structure. Although STP really impacts the family, it can also impact the business on various levels. Potential non-family leaders—especially the strong, thoughtful candidates—frequently want to understand if the owners share a common vision for the business. In addition, banking relationships can be strengthened when clear alignment of shareholders can be demonstrated through STP structures, thus reducing the chances of family turmoil negatively impacting the operations of the family business. A stable ownership structure can contribute to a stable family business.

Questions related to STP include:
- Is there a risk that ownership in your family business will be highly fragmented in the future so no one person or small group is in control of shareholder decisions?
- Is the future ownership of your family company clearly defined? How will shares pass through future generations in various family branches? Is there a consistent plan across family branches?

- Do you have a Family/Corporate Governance Plan? In other words, do you have rules governing ownership such as outright ownership, ownership in trusts, or requirements for estate planning to avoid unexpected estate taxes associated with the ownership of the family business?

- Do you have an ownership transition plan in place that all family members understand? Does the company do any education around estate planning? And do they support family members in this process?

- If you died unexpectedly, would your business have to be sold to pay estate taxes? Or would redemptions to pay estate taxes cripple capital expenditures?

- Do you complete regular valuations of your business to facilitate gifting shares to the next generation?

- Are shares of the business required to be held in trusts to avoid probate, which could lead to the value of the company becoming part of the public record for your competitors to see?

- Much has been written elsewhere about BSP, and very little about STP. For our purposes, the majority of our discussion in this book will be about STP, and specifically how an FTC facilitates the transition that helps business owners, I hope, lose a lot less sleep.

Meet the Owners

Throughout this book I will try to illustrate key concepts with examples from families that have dealt with the same challenges faced by countless family-business owners. These case studies are based on actual families, but many of the details have been changed to protect the privacy of the family and their business operations.

G1, G2, G3

I will be referring to family members by their generational relationships. Business founders, or the wealth creators, are the first generation, or G1; their children are G2, which is frequently led by one child, often called The Benevolent Dictator who the other siblings defer to; and the grandchildren, at times referred to as the Cousin Consortium, are G3. The great-grandchildren of the founder(s) are G4, and so on.

G1 Wealth Creator: Ed

As the sole owner of a successful business, Ed is a G1 wealth creator. Ed has spent most of his life focused on building the business without fully realizing the magnitude of wealth he's been creating, nor taking the time to build structures around supporting his family in keeping the family business within the family. He believes the business model will allow the enterprise to continue to grow into the foreseeable future, continuing to provide financial freedom for his children—and hopefully his grandchildren, too.

Ed is widowed with two minor children, Matt and Laura. One thing that keeps Ed up at night is: Who will help guide his children and oversee their interest in the business in the future—or sooner if he passes away unexpectedly? Currently, he does have a number of trusted advisors, but it is important to Ed that his children understand the business regardless if in the future they choose to work in the business or not.

G2 Patriarch: David

The sibling leader of G2 can also encounter sleepless nights. David is the eldest son of the wealth creator with four siblings, each of whom have worked, or currently work, in the business. This sibling group spent many nights at dinner with their "boots under the same table" hearing their parents talk about the stresses—and blood, sweat and tears—their parents were expressing through the growth phases of a now very successful family business. David and each of his siblings also worked in the family business at some time—even if just for a summer job.

G1 has passed away and the siblings have inherited ownership of the family business. Since then, the business has continued to be very successful, with family members in the second and third generations taking active roles in the business. However, only a few G3 family members have joined the business, unlike the G2 family members who have worked in the business.

What keeps David up at night is that one—or worse, multiple—untimely sibling deaths could result in personal representatives of the G2 siblings' estates asking for redemptions of shares to meet estate tax obligations on the illiquid ownership of the business.

Reluctant to give up control, the G2 siblings have not done estate planning to pass shares of the family business on to G3 family members. And they worry that as the family becomes larger, the family's values, traditions, and overall commitment to the business are being weakened. Since all of the boots aren't under the same table for dinner, how can they at least get all of the boots under the same roof?

G3 Cousins: Fred, Sandy, and Dale

For the families that make it to the Cousin Consortium era—the G3 grandchildren now are in charge—new challenges arise as fewer and fewer family members make the decision to work in the family business. Over time, the sheer number of cousins, spousal influence with different perspectives and values, and geographical dispersion strain the ties that bind owners of family businesses.

Fred, Sandy, and Dale are all G3s who work for the family business and want to see the business remain family owned. They all share a passion and connection to the G1 legacy and want to preserve it. Sandy is the eldest cousin, Dale is the youngest cousin, and Fred is married to a G3. There are 14 G3s, including spouses.

These G3 family members are kept up at night wondering how the many cousins—most of whom don't work in the business—will make shareholder decisions together in the best interest of the family business. They wonder:

- How should family members working in the business be treated differently than those not working in the business?
- How to educate G3s that don't work in the business so they can make informed shareholder decisions?
- How can they ensure the cousins working outside the business continue their emotional commitment to the family business?
- How do they separate succession planning decisions (who runs the business) from shareholder transition decisions (who and how is the company owned)?
- What role, if any, do spouses play in the family enterprise?

As you can see, as the number of family members increase across generations, there are more questions with increasing complexity with widely varying perspectives resulting in the potential for many more sleepless nights.

CHAPTER 2

Family Businesses: Engines of the U.S. Economy

WITHOUT A DOUBT, family businesses play a vital role as engines of the U.S. economy. With a wave of baby boomers reaching retirement age and a substantial wealth transfer on the horizon, the need for effective shareholder transitions in family enterprises is becoming ever more pressing. However, in spite of this trend, many family businesses lack comprehensive shareholder transition plans. To address these challenges, we'll look deeper into the concept of a family trust company as a potential integral player in the solution. We'll also examine, through family-business case studies, the repercussions of inadequate planning.

Family Businesses Today

A Deeper Question

There are many reasons clients or their advisors contact me to learn more about utilizing FTCs for shareholder transitions. Some questions are driven by the fact that more than 10,000 baby boomers are turning 65 every day, with trillions of dollars of wealth to be transferred over the next 20 to 30 years.[2] Baby Boomers are actively thinking about the legacy they want to leave and how to perpetuate their family values into the future.

With ever increasing frequency, the concern over estate tax issues is rearing its head, particularly when family members take a moment to project the value of the company in three, five, or seven years. This simple exercise in planning can highlight the need to minimize any estate tax due at the family member's death that could jeopardize the business staying privately held by the family.

When families want to keep the business in the family, the question becomes how to pass shares to future generations in a way to help keep the family harmonized. But this question also covers other equally significant concerns, such as communicating and passing on family values, keeping the family cohesive and working together for generations, and preparing successive generations to take over the business or be good stewards of the company. Families need to proactively work on keeping the family together. It is not a passive activity.

A family business is more than its quantifiable parts. Yes, family enterprises are in business to make a profit. But what truly drives many family businesses is the sense of connection and identity the owners and their family members feel with the business itself. Family businesses regularly outperform their public counterparts over time because families may have more tolerance to weather the inevitable storm that the family business encounters. Management doesn't have to answer to a sea of faceless shareholders who may be solely motivated by the size of the profit. Most families truly care about the family business and its long-term success in addition to the employees that help propel the business forward. "While public companies are up against quarterly results and the demand for short-term profitability, family businesses have the luxury of putting long-term values over short-term gains. We can embrace strategies that put customers and employees first and emphasize social responsibility," says family business expert Mitzi Perdue.[3]

Family Case: David, G2 Patriarch

Consider David's story from earlier. As the G2 "Benevolent Dictator" and CEO of the family business, he spent years focusing on growing the company. And growth had been fast and furious, which at times was all-consuming. He and his siblings were all engaged in the business and hadn't paused to think about the implication of estate taxes. David would say that estate taxes were "out of their wheelhouse" while also being out of their comfort zone. Talking about your passing and what happens when you are no longer in control can be a difficult conversation. It took a life-threatening emergency for a younger sibling to push David to reach out to his advisors asking about options to start to transition shares to future generations.

During an early educational session of the shareholder transition options, David was encouraged to do a quick calculation with the value of the shares projected out over five years, based on the growth the company was experiencing and believed would continue. This simple exercise greatly surprised David, as it became apparent that within five years all of the siblings would be facing significant estate tax obligations. None of the siblings had an abundance of liquid assets saved, with most of their wealth tied up in shares of the company, which issued very little dividends because funds were continually plowed back into the business to feed its rapid growth. They all were wealthy on paper, but with limited funds to pay the looming estate tax bills, they were facing a crisis.

David now realized how important planning for the family (shareholder transition) needed to be just as important as planning for company leadership (business succession). Up to this point, he had spent significant time and thoughtfulness on business succession, but no time on developing a shareholder transition vision. He quickly became the visionary for the shareholder transition process wanting to understand various options available to his siblings and how they could become aligned. They were able to rely on the shared history with boots under the same table to come to agreement on creating Dynasty Trusts with an FTC at the helm as trustee of each of their trusts.

Wealth holders and business owners want to transfer not only their wealth but also their values, such as encouraging children to earn their own money, and participate in philanthropy, charitable giving, and volunteering.[4]

"Shirtsleeves to Shirtsleeves"

Back to the proverbial saying, it is interesting to note that the average age of family control in the family's core company is 60.2 years.[5] While more than 30 percent of all family-owned businesses survive into the second generation, only 12 percent will be still viable into the third, and a meager 3 percent of all family businesses operate at the fourth-generation level and beyond.[6]

Family Businesses: Engines of the U.S. Economy

Why is this scenario repeated over and over again to the point of being considered the norm? The first generation founds the business and works hard to grow it; the second generation are direct witnesses to the efforts, sacrifices, knowledge and lessons of the first generation. As alluded to in the introduction to G2 David's case above, it's not unusual that nightly dinner conversation would revolve around the journey of the business thus the saying they have their "boots under the same table." I've heard a family business referred to as the "other sibling" since it was so integral to family discussions. But the third generation grows up with an established business as the normal condition of their lives and are not necessarily direct witnesses to its growth and management. And likely they are not witnesses to the roller coaster of trial and error that can be the norm of the early days. The family grows with each generation and becomes more dispersed, geographically and with that its ability to transmit the core values of the founders.

Everything becomes more difficult, especially if you don't have a plan. Remember, too, their boots aren't under the same table anymore, nor even under the same roof. A visionary perspective becomes imperative. As so aptly stated by entrepreneur Richard Seaman, "A business owner must from the outset make a decision about the long-term vision for the business, because strategic decisions for the business will vary depending on that long-term vision."[7] I would add that a long-term vision for the *family* is as important as a long-term vision for the business.

Research suggests that 70 percent of all wealth transfer plans fail.[8] Babetta von Albertini, Co-Founder and Chair of the Institute for Family Governance (IFG), says, "When evaluating these failed plans, 60 percent are due to breakdown of trust and communication in the family, and an additional 25 percent are due to a failure to prepare the next generation for what's to come."

Business owners need to be proactive about planning for the family business future. If you don't have a plan, the government—both federal and your state—has one for you. And the longer you wait, the greater the complexities—the multitude of spouses, children, grandchildren and assets—and the greater the challenges are of communicating effectively to the whole family.

Family Businesses Know How to do Business Right

Family businesses leaders focus on the next generation, not the next quarter. They value continuity and not outside shareholders. They tend to embrace strategies that put customers and employees first and emphasize social responsibility.[9] But they face big issues, as well. According to the 2019 Deloitte family business survey, while almost half of respondents listed "continuing family legacy and tradition" as the most important non-economic goal of the company over the coming year, only 18 percent indicated that succession planning was one of their top two priorities, and only 26 percent had a formal plan in place for the CEO position. Even fewer had plans for executive positions other than the CEO.[10] And the Business Succession Plan is typically the first to be considered, with the Shareholder Transition Plan a distant second.

Interestingly, banks working with family businesses are often just as interested in the Shareholder Transition Plan as they are in the Business Succession Plan. Particularly when family businesses are in the third generation and beyond, banks are more interested in how the shares are held, and is the family harmonized in its commitment to continuing as a family-owned business. It can alleviate the bank's concerns of redemption requests pulling on the company's bottom line. Filling key employee positions as part of the Business Succession Plan can also be easier when the family can share a thoughtful, positive ownership structure standing behind the company.

Strong job candidates are likely to ask about the ownership structure and how the family works together as part of the interview process. The answers to these questions can help land the right talent. The potential employee wants to know how stable the ownership structure is, as that brings career implications for the executive team. Knowing a family has thoughtfully structured ownership and put in place a shareholder decision process can go a long way in securing talent at a time when talent is at a premium.

The reality is that owners will eventually leave the business, whether they retire or pass away while at the helm of their business, creating a period of chaos as to the destiny of the family business. Sometimes this is called the DIP plan—or Die In Place plan—which isn't an effective plan for the business nor the family. According to The National Center for the Middle Market, nearly three-quarters of business in their survey plan to transition in the next five years.[11]

Yet two-thirds of owners do not have a clear retirement plan, and just over half do not have a succession plan. This is in line with results from the 2022 Mass Mutual® Business Owner Perspectives Study showing that 67 percent of business owners have not identified a successor.[12]

Family Businesses are Economic Powerhouses

Keeping family businesses together across generations is important for the economy. Family businesses drive local, national, and global economies. They account for 64 percent of the U.S. GDP, generate 62 percent of the country's employment, account for 78 percent of new job creation, and comprise the greatest part of America's wealth—80 to 90 percent.[13] Family businesses retain talent better than their competitors do: only 9 percent of their work forces turned over annually (versus 11 percent at non-family firms). They create a culture of commitment and purpose, avoiding layoffs during downturns, promoting from within, and investing in people.[14] That's a heck of a lot to leave to chance, changing circumstances, growing numbers of family members, and changing fortunes in the marketplace.

Why is Transition Planning Hard?

Letting go is difficult—for many reasons. Owners may not know what they would do if they aren't working in the business—an effort that has given them a sense of mission for years, even decades. They may be concerned the next generation isn't ready yet or are waiting for younger family members to come into the business or for potential successors to speak up and demand ownership. An owner may want just one more challenge or new product before they address transition. Or they believe they can remain in charge indefinitely, and are defaulting to the DIP (Die in Place) plan.

Then there are the not inconsequential matters of how the owner will continue to receive an income stream, plus differences in shareholder expectations surrounding any transition plans. But waiting and doing nothing does not make these issues go away. It's worth revisiting some of our questions from earlier:

- Would your business be able to survive if you were disabled? If so, for how long?
- If you unexpectedly died, would your business have to be sold to pay estate taxes?
- Is there a second-in-command (family or non-family) who you are grooming, or have plans to develop?
- Are there objective criteria to evaluate the strengths, weaknesses, skills and talents of any family members working in the business?

Simply waiting isn't going to make your successors, or your business, more ready. It's important to consider these important questions—and to discuss them with the family so everyone in the boat is rowing together. Remember, breakdown of communication and trust within the family is a key factor in wealth transfer plans that fail.

Importance of Family Company Dynamics

Each family member who is working in the business has a role and status as an employee. And most likely some other family members might have ownership but are not be working in the business. Further complicating the structure could be current and former spouses, brothers, sisters, aunts, uncles, grandparents, and so on who have some influence on the business and ownership through family structure, relationships, and dynamics. Even if a spouse does not have ownership, they have influence and expectations through the family member that does have ownership.

Roles and priorities in family companies are subject to many kinds of conflict and misunderstandings. It's important to understand the nuances of intersection of these overlapping relationships—owners, family, and family members working in the business.

Only 35 percent of respondents to the 2019 Deloitte Family Business Survey agreed that the company's long-term plan was aligned with the objectives of the business as well as with all family members' individual and shared goals. And families seem to be growing larger and more complex; and events such as death, marriage, divorce as well as disputes create the potential for severe disruption.[15]

Where Family Trust Companies Come In

FTCs specifically address these important questions of continuity, stewardship, communication, engagement, ownership, and values.

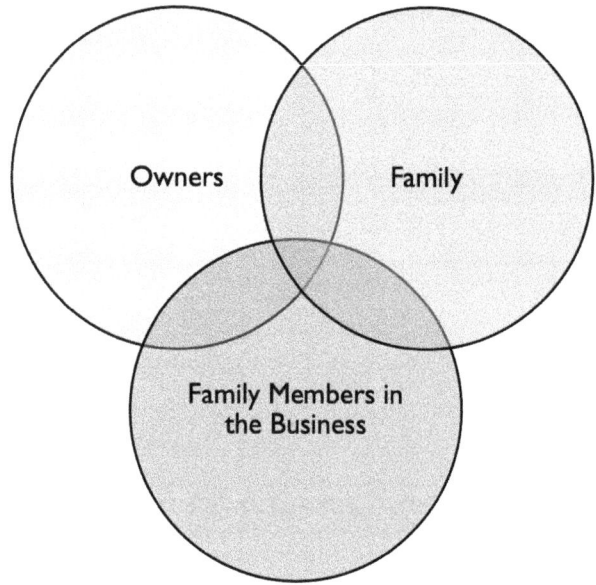

Under an FTC, families maintain control over strategic assets and decisions, manage fiduciary liability, and embed their mission and values into a formal structure that survives for generations. Best of all, FTCs are applicable to a range of families including families with a family businesses or families that have experienced a liquidity event. In addition, FTCs are flexible enough to adapt to the family's changing needs over time.

Importantly, FTCs help to formalize the structure of the ownership of the business moving forward and make the situation clear for everyone—embracing those key components of strengthening communication and building trust. Governance and decision-making procedures can be objective and transparent. We can bring all those boots—as diverse and geographically dispersed as they may be—back under the same roof.

Insufficient Plans: Three Family Cases

What are the risks of not planning? We'll start by looking at common scenarios involving families that faced the consequences of inadequate planning.

Family Case: Ed and an Unplanned Transition

Remember Ed, our widowed G1 wealth creator with two minor children? His relentless focus on growing the company brought him a comfortable lifestyle, but amidst the hustle and bustle of entrepreneurship, he never fully grasped the magnitude of the wealth he was accumulating, nor did he establish the necessary structures to ensure a seamless transition of his legacy to the next generation. He hadn't taken the time to complete a thoughtful estate plan nor select advisors that would be able to support his children if he wasn't here to guide them.

Tragedy strikes when Ed unexpectedly passes away, leaving behind a business owned outright with minimal estate planning completed and a looming estate tax bill. The ownership of his company is divided into two segments: a small portion held in trust for his children, Matt and Laura, and a majority directly inherited by them with control turned over to the children when they each turn 18. By default, when not held in a trust, inherited assets distribute the moment children reach the age of majority, which is 18 in most states. Thankfully, the company has a strong leadership team, as Ed did think about succession planning. So, the right people were in the right seats to keep the company moving forward and growing. With a large portion of the company included in Ed's estate, the company did take a hit to its capital expenditure budget when it had to redeem shares from Ed's estate to cover the estate tax bill, but fortunately the company was able to manage this unexpected event without selling the company or any portion of the company. Therefore, the ownership ultimately remained with Matt and Laura.

When Matt and Laura each turn 18 and take the reins of their newfound wealth, they follow drastically different paths. Laura, lured by the pull of newfound riches, splurges on extravagant purchases like an expensive show horse and globe-trotting adventures. However, as she quickly depletes the ready liquidity she has, she returns to the company seeking additional funds. Tensions rise as redeeming shares becomes the only option to fund her extravagant lifestyle, thus disrupting the company's management and its growth trajectory. Members of the strong leadership team also start to consider leaving the company for new opportunities as they question the long-term viability of the company given Laura's lack of interest in the company's growth and her apparent need for cash.

Matt, driven by a deep sense of responsibility and a desire to preserve his father's legacy, is committed to keeping the company intact and resists any attempts to sell any portion of the company. The conflict between the two siblings escalates to a point where they can barely communicate, resorting to the use of a mediator. Simultaneously, Matt is trying to calm the concerns of the company's leadership team asking for time to deal with Laura.

Finally, the impending storm of probate litigation looms large, threatening to tear the siblings and company apart. Matt is torn between honoring his father's legacy and dealing with the chaos ensuing from the inheritance based on his father's lack of planning. The entire situation becomes a quagmire of familial strife and legal complexities. Company leaders are also starting to defect with a key employee leaving for a position at a more stable company.

Adding to the turmoil is the fear of the individual trustee of the trust holding a portion of the company. This individual trustee is responsible for managing the trust's assets and his fiduciary liability is not only to both current beneficiaries, Laura and Matt, but to their potential children, if there are no assets left in the trust. The trust assets are highly concentrated in the family business, and trustees are typically bound by a fiduciary duty to prudently diversify the assets. Laura, seeking more liquidity from the trust, pushes for diversification with assets paying dividends to fund her lifestyle, which would inevitably result in selling a portion of the company, further fueling the conflict.

In this tragic case, Ed's failure to engage in comprehensive estate planning and provide guidance for the next generation's wealth management has unleashed a storm of disputes and instability within the family and the company that he built with his grit and determination. The absence of a well-thought-out shareholder transition plan and trust structures has turned what should have been a smooth transfer of the company into a family crisis.

Family Case: G3 Cousins and a Lucrative Proposition

Now let's turn to the G3 cousins Fred, Sandy, and Dale. There is a new reason for sleepless nights for these three; the company has received a lucrative offer to sell the company. Fred, Sandy, and Dale have always worried about their G3 cousins, each hailing from diverse backgrounds and career paths, when faced with a tempting prospect of liquidity. How will they come together as a coordinated group to decide whether to sell or not, and if so at what price?

With minimal estate planning that would have placed the ownership of the company in trusts overseen by a trustee, ownership of the company is held outright by the various shareholders. This will require consensus to be reached among individuals with varying financial situations, associated spousal influence, and familial ties to the company. The consequences of this decision weigh heavily on their shoulders as they also think about what will happen to the employees of the company who have become their teammates and friends. Accepting the offer would potentially bring substantial financial gains to the family owners, but it could also signify the end of an era, marking the departure from their family's entrepreneurial legacy. While rejecting the offer would commit them to the responsibilities and uncertainties of continued family ownership with an ever-expanding disbursement of ownership as G3s gift shares of the company to their children: G4.

Spread across different corners of the country, the G3 cousins faced the logistical challenge of finding a common ground to discuss the future before embarking on trying to build consensus. The consequences of this geographical dispersion are tangible—scheduling meetings that accommodated everyone's time zones and availability has become an intricate puzzle. While virtual meetings help bridge the physical gaps, the challenge remains in achieving a shared perspective and understanding.

Those that work in the company have a better understanding of the company's current financial state as well as its future growth opportunities. Some G3 family members may view the family business as a legacy asset that has great emotional ties, while others may consider the family business simply a financial asset and are concerned primarily about its monetary return. Bringing all of these perspectives together and overlaying them with the family's values becomes more challenging over space and time.

Within this intricate web of family dynamics, one cousin's spouse has emerged as an influential figure. With a penchant for numbers and a relentless quest for information, this spouse has demanded transparency from the management, sometimes even overshadowing the voices of the G3 cousins. The consequences are palpable, as the intrusion of a non-blood family member adds complexity to the decision-making process. Striking the right balance between involving spouses and preserving the core family's decision-making authority have become a contentious issue, risking further divisions within the family.

As the cousins reflect on this tumultuous journey, they begin to wonder: Could there have been a better way? An FTC could have acted as a unifying and professional force, providing guidance, expertise, and structure to the decision-making process. This would have alleviated many of the challenges and tensions faced by the G3 cousins, making it easier for them to navigate the complexities of preserving their family business while still having the ability to consider the offer to purchase and other critical issues.

Family Case: A Tragedy for G2

David, our G2 Benevolent Dictator and CEO, was laser-focused on the company's growth. However, amidst their pursuit of excellence, the family overlooked a crucial aspect—estate planning. Then, when two siblings, traveling together, die enroute to a crucial family meeting the family is plunged into grief. Without warning, the company, thus the family, is also thrust into an immediate financial crisis.

The family neglected to move assets out of G2s' estates. As a result, it became painfully evident that they did not do adequate planning because the G2s who passed have estates facing substantial estate taxes based on their illiquid company ownership. Not surprisingly, the Executors of these estates were turning to the company asking for shares to be redeemed to assist in the payment of the estate taxes. The size of the necessary redemptions would threaten the business' existence—or require a sale of the business to raise the liquidity. Estate planning, once an abstract notion, had turned into a grim reality. Desperate to resolve mounting estate tax liabilities, the family had to consider selling a significant part of the company or even all of the company—their life's work and shared dreams. This was an emotionally charged, gut-wrenching choice.

This unexpected tragedy served as a reminder of the critical role of thoughtful estate planning for shareholders in family-owned businesses. It emphasized that the ideal time to prepare for the future is always the present.

CHAPTER 3

A Deeper Dive into FTCs

FTCs, OFTEN REFERRED to as private trust companies in some states, represent an innovative and family-centric approach to wealth management. These entities have gained prominence with increasing momentum in recent years as a powerful tool for preserving and managing the wealth of affluent families across generations. An FTC, in essence, is a privately-owned and -controlled entity with a singular mission: acting as a fiduciary such as a trustee to oversee assets for the exclusive benefit of a single-family lineage for those assets held in trusts. FTCs are authorized by state statute so they can only be set up in certain states. Ohio is one of the states along with South Dakota, Wyoming, Nevada, Tennessee, among others.[16]

Even though the FTC's services are limited to a single-family lineage, most families pick an ancestor that when considering the ancestor's lineal descendants, the FTC ultimately serves multiple family branches. For example, to ensure the FTC can serve all family shareholders of a multigenerational family business, the FTC may be set up to serve the family lineage of the great-grandfather that started the business (or back further if there are more family branches with ownership).

Basically, the FTC becomes the corporate trustee for trusts set up by or for family members. It cannot hold itself out to the public or offer services to non-family clients. The FTC may not provide some banking services such as mortgages or hold deposits. Trusts of which the FTC is trustee can make loans to beneficiaries but the FTC itself cannot loan money. While this background provides a foundational understanding, the intricacies of FTCs warrant loser examination.

In this thorough exploration of FTCs, each element of the definition, as well as other features, will be explored highlighting their unique features and the critical role they play in multi-generational wealth management and legacy preservation.

Family-Owned and -Controlled Entity: The Essence of FTCs

At the core of an FTC lies the principle of family ownership and control—in fact it is required by law. This is a defining characteristic that sets FTCs apart from traditional corporate trustees or financial institutions. An FTC is not a faceless entity; it's an organization intrinsically linked to the family it serves. Family members own the FTC. Family members collaborating with trusted advisors possessing specialized expertise, control the FTC through serving on the Board and various committees to make strategic decisions.

These familial connections ensure that the decision-making process remains firmly aligned with the family. Every strategic choice reflects the family's values, aspirations, and collective vision for their wealth strategy including the family business. The FTC structure has enough flexibility that it can also evolve over time to reflect the generational changes and perspectives that occur over time. The family is firmly at the helm of making decisions about its wealth strategy and shareholder decisions for the family business.

The family determines how the FTC will support the family through any services it offers. The family determines what committees should be formed to support the family. The family determines what trusted advisors to sit alongside the family to support the family on the Board or a committee of the FTC. Although the FTC is a fiduciary responsible for the oversight of assets in the family trusts, it can also be set up to support the family offering select family office services. Moreover, since the family exercises direct influence over the services the FTC provides, the family directly determines the entity's budget and operational scope. This puts the family in control of the ongoing operational costs of the FTC. Typically, a budget is created that encompasses director fees, any insurance premiums, educational programming, and family engagement activities, to name a few. Once the budget is developed, trustee fees are determined and allocated to the trusts under the management of the FTC to cover the expenses. Although the FTC isn't intended to lose money, it also doesn't have a large profit motive as it is not being used as a wealth transfer vehicle. Unlike institutional corporate trustees, the goal isn't to make a large profit. Therefore, an FTC can be a very cost-effective corporate trustee option.

This familial ownership and control are pivotal in sculpting an FTC's character. The intimate involvement of the family on the FTC's Board and committees can engender a sense of trust, fostering an environment where financial decisions are guided by a shared purpose and a deep understanding of the family's dynamics. Family members who work together get to know each other through building stronger connections which can enhance trust among family members and foster a shared family purpose.

Sole Purpose: A Laser-Focused Mandate

Unlike traditional financial institutions that engage in a broad spectrum of financial and commercial activities, an FTC maintains its focus on acting as a fiduciary for the family. It does not extend its services to the general public, hold deposits, or provide mortgages. With this mandate, the FTC can offer highly personalized, family-centric services while remaining aware of the family's culture and dynamics. This focused approach allows the FTC to tailor its offerings to align with the family's distinct objectives and values.

In essence, the "sole purpose" principle safeguards the family's control over its wealth strategy and the direction of its legacy. The FTC can be uniquely structured to have concentrated decision makers over various family decisions by family members with the most comprehensive understanding of the family and family business. For example, a Family Business Asset Committee can be set up with members having a background in the family business so they are best situated to make shareholder decisions related to the family business. As another example, an Education Committee can be established and populated with parents focused on ensuring the next generation (their children) develops into good stewards of the family's wealth. Resources can be dedicated to not only the family's financial well-being, but its human, intellectual and spiritual capital as well.

Management of Assets: Safeguarding Family Wealth

An FTC functions as guardian of the family trusts set up over time, with each successive generation becoming beneficiaries of an ever-growing web of trusts holding the family wealth and family business. These assets can encompass a wide array of investments, ranging from family businesses and marketable securities to real estate holdings and more. Frequently, the overarching objective is not only to preserve these assets but also to foster their growth over time, ensuring their enduring utility for the benefit of family beneficiaries spanning multiple generations. At the same time, the family involvement in the FTC serves to encourage the stewardship of the family's wealth supported by additional education and increased transparency which can engender trust amongst family members.

The management of assets held in the family trusts entails a multifaceted approach that combines financial stewardship with an understanding of the family's unique goals and risk tolerance. Asset diversification, risk management, and tax optimization are among the strategies employed by the FTC to ensure the assets flourish over time—or the goal may be to hold the family business as a privately held enterprise across the next generation. Family members may contribute their intellectual capital to the oversight of the assets in the trusts under the management of the FTC, family members can learn alongside trusted advisors with the required expertise or operational functions of the FTC can be outsourced leaving the family members to be the guiding decision-makers with outsourced providers executing on behalf of the family (e.g., investment services, trust administration support or tax planning). The key here is that the family makes the decisions on what the family wants to do and when they would like to oversee an outsourced provider.

Furthermore, the FTC's role extends beyond mere asset management. It involves developing the strategic vision for the family, providing consistent reporting, and transmitting regular communication with family members to ensure that everyone remains informed.

Benefit of a Single-Family Lineage: Defining the Family

As previously mentioned, the family determines the individual—called the Designated Relative in Ohio—as the starting point in determining the family lineage served. In addition, under Ohio law, the single family lineage comprises a comprehensive range of family members, including spouses, spousal equivalents, former spouses, children, adopted children, step-children, and foster children. However, the scope of beneficiaries served by the FTC can vary based on state law and the family's preferences. For example, some families prefer not to serve former spouses due to the family dynamics that can be created around these situations.

States like Ohio extend this definition even further to include family charitable beneficiaries, key employees, family estates, trusts established for family members, entities owned and operated by family members, and more. This expansive view provides families with the flexibility to define the boundaries of their lineage according to their unique circumstances and objectives.

Families can choose to commence with a living family elder as the Designated Relative, effectively limiting the lineage to initially just two or three generations. Alternatively, they may trace their lineage back several generations, substantially expanding the pool of eligible family members served. This flexibility allows the family to create an FTC that is precisely tailored to the needs and aspirations of the family lineage.

Customized and Centralized Control Over Family Trusts: Navigating Complexity

One of the best features of an FTC is that it delivers consistent, customized and centralized management of the family trusts. Beneficiaries receive the same information as determined by the family and state statutes. Over time, beneficiaries embark on divergent paths, pursuing varying careers, residing in different geographical locations, and establishing unique nuclear family units, all of which can significantly influence their financial landscapes, but they are all still served by the FTC.

As families grow across generations, it is common that a single trust document provides that the assets held in the trust are divided into separate trusts for the succeeding generations. That means at each generation, more trusts are created that, without careful planning, result in multiplying the number of trustees with the responsibility to manage the family's assets. For a family business, with numerous and diverse trustees, it could result in lots of inquiries about the company's performance as well as varying demands on the return on the investment in the family business. The FTC centralizes the trustee perspective when it becomes the trustee of most, if not all, of the family trusts. Rather than an ever-increasing pool of trustees with varying knowledge of the family's values and family business, ownership in the family business can be held by the FTC with oversight by family members and trusted advisors. This can be game-changing for a family business with ownership at the G3 level given by this stage, fewer family members work in the business, spousal influence becomes more evident and geographical disbursement has set in.

An FTC's role extends beyond the traditional oversight of assets in the trusts. The team comprising the Board and various committees can become trusted advisors, offering comprehensive guidance and mentorship. Ideally, the members of the Discretionary Distribution Committee (more later on this committee) are independent advisors who come to know the beneficiaries well—understanding their aspirations and how distributions from the trust can enhance the life of a beneficiary. This holistic approach ensures that the family's wealth is not merely preserved but optimized to support the diverse needs and goals of beneficiaries across generations.

As noted previously, transparency and communication have been shown to be characteristics of families that continue to thrive across generations. The FTC can ensure that, as appropriate, family beneficiaries receive consistent and transparent information.

This uniformity and openness are invaluable in preventing potential misunderstandings and misinformation that can arise when different trustees provide varying information to different family beneficiaries. It is human nature to "fill in the gaps" if you aren't provided with information—unfortunately the suspected information is rarely correct.

Setting Up an FTC: Navigating the Nuances

To gain a comprehensive understanding of FTCs, it is essential to delve into the operational mechanics that can govern these entities. Let's explore the key elements that define how an FTC is set up.

Legal Framework and Regulatory Compliance

The establishment and operation of an FTC are subject to specific legal requirements to ensure compliance with state law plus IRS and SEC guidance. These requirements can vary depending on the state in which the FTC is formed. An important consideration in determining the jurisdiction for forming the FTC is the family's interest in a regulated (licensed) versus unregulated (unlicensed) environment. Some states only offer regulated FTCs while some states, including Ohio, offer both licensed (regulated) and unlicensed (unregulated) options. The difference is licensed FTCs are subject to regular procedural audits by the state's banking regulators. There may also be specific activities required by the state and additional fees associated with the state's regulation. Travel to the state where the FTC is established is also important to protect the FTC's jurisdiction and application of that state law. Time, travel complexity, and budget constraints shouldn't be ignored.

Another consideration is the capital requirement to set up an FTC. This requirement varies significantly by state. Regulated trust companies have a specific dollar amount as a statutory capital requirement, or as determined by the state banking regulator in some states. For example, Ohio's licensed FTC capital requirement is between $200,000 to $500,000, as determined by the banking regulator. Ohio unlicensed FTCs are not governed by this same requirement.

Regulated trust companies also have an application process including an associated application fee. The application must be approved by the banking regulators prior to the FTC commencing operations. This adds expense, time and complexity to the set up. Unregulated trust companies typically have minimal, if any, oversight from the state banking regulators. Ohio's only state statutory requirement for an unlicensed FTC is to annually file an affidavit stating that the FTC meets the statutory requirements to qualify to act as an unlicensed FTC.

It is imperative for families contemplating the creation of an FTC to engage legal counsel with expertise in the relevant jurisdiction to ensure full compliance with all legal and regulatory prerequisites. And always, it is important to remember that the FTC is a fiduciary in its capacity as a trust company.

Board of Directors and Governance

Frequently, an FTC is governed by a Board of Directors and supported by committees. The Board of Directors is composed of family members and trusted advisors. If properly set up, grantors of the family trusts as well as beneficiaries may serve on the

Board and most committees. The Board is responsible for shaping the policies, strategies, and operational framework of the FTC as well as ensuring decisions are guided by the family's values. The Board also names Officers of the FTC who assist in the operations of the FTC and implement decisions made by the Board or a Committee. Officers don't have to be on the Board nor do they have to be family members.

Family members on the Board bring an intimate understanding of the family's dynamics and long-term vision. Trusted advisors, on the other hand, contribute specialized expertise in financial management, trust administration, legal matters, and taxation. The trusted advisors usually have known or worked with the family over time—sometimes in the capacity of an individual trustee of family trusts. They can bring a historical perspective and institutional knowledge to the table imparting it to the next generation as well. This combination of familial insight, history and technical proficiency ensures that the FTC operates effectively in alignment with the family's objectives.

Specific functions of the FTC can be managed within unique committees. Committees can be comprised of directors, but also non-directors who bring specific knowledge to the Committee. These committees can address specific aspects of trust and wealth management, such as investment oversight, distribution decisions, education planning or family engagement. Through the FTC's corporate documents, committees can also be set up to maintain privacy and confidentiality regarding decisions related to specific beneficiaries. This can be very important when considering distribution decisions.

Operational Budget and Service Offerings

As highlighted earlier, another area the family is in control is determining the operational budget of the FTC which is directly related to its service offerings. Unlike traditional financial institutions driven by profit margins for external stakeholders, the family determines the appropriate expenditures for the FTC adding on a small profit margin for unexpected items. Some items driving the size of the budget include director fees, travel expenses, D&O insurance, and family education programs. In determining these amounts, here are some questions to consider:

- Will family Directors receive compensation for serving on the FTC Board?

- How much is the family willing to pay Independent Directors to serve on the FTC Board to benefit from their expertise?

- How large is the Board?

- Who needs to attend the FTC meetings in person to drive the travel budget?

- What family expenses will be covered when a Family Director attends an FTC meeting?

- Will, and how much, D&O insurance will be required by the jurisdiction state or needed to attract the appropriate Independent Directors?

- Will there be any educational opportunities for directors or for beneficiaries (e.g., attending conferences, bringing in speakers, etc.)?

- In addition to fiduciary services as trustee, will the FTC offer any more traditional family office services?
- What services will the family perform and what services will be outsourced?

As you can see, each FTC's budget can be tailored based on a wide range of decisions. Fees specifically related to an individual trust (e.g., tax preparation of a trust tax return) are typically charged to the individual trust so not part of the FTC's operational budget.

Wealth Transfer and Shareholder Transition Planning

An FTC can play an integral role in wealth transfer and shareholder transition planning. As the consistent trustee across family trusts, it facilitates an orderly transition of assets from one generation to the next, ensuring that the family's wealth or family business endures intergenerationally. After an entrepreneur builds a business, it can be very difficult to transition ownership to the next generation. Knowing, as the grantor of a trust holding family-business ownership, the grantor can still have a seat at the table to discuss shareholder decisions, it eases this transition. Many times, especially for family-business owners, doing estate planning can be stalled when the trustee decision must be made to complete the documents. Giving up dominion and control is hard, but the structure of the FTC can provide comfort that family members will continue at the helm of shareholder decisions with the grantor also part of the decision-making process.

Confidentiality and Privacy

One of the reasons families have historically used individual trustees as trustees for family trusts is in addition to being very familiar with the family, it reduces outsider knowledge of the family's wealth or details of the family business. These families have avoided using large, institutional trustees to keep things "all in the family."

An FTC considers confidentiality and privacy from two perspectives—external knowledge and intrafamily knowledge. The FTC operates within a secure and confidential environment where sensitive family information is safeguarded. This ensures that family affairs remain private, avoiding public probate proceedings or undue exposure of financial details. Certain decisions related to specific beneficiaries can also be kept confidential with ratification of decisions by the Board not required.

The Role of an FTC in Multigenerational Wealth Management: A Holistic Approach

The role of an FTC in multigenerational wealth management can encompass a holistic approach. Let's delve deeper into the multifaceted role an FTC can serve in nurturing a family across generations.

Preservation of Family Values

An FTC operates as a custodian of family values even though it can't physically custody the financial assets. It can strive to integrate the family's core principles and values into the trustee/beneficiary relationship through services offered, education programs provided, mentoring opportunities, and more. The FTC can be designed to support the family's human capital along with its financial capital. This approach can help move a family business asset from being viewed purely as a financial asset with an expected return to a legacy asset resulting in a stewardship view. Many families I work with carefully consider the characteristics of those serving on the Board or committees then outline these characteristics in the FTC's governing documents.

Facilitation of Philanthropic Endeavors

For some families, the FTC plays a pivotal role in facilitating the family's philanthropic endeavors, even if it doesn't act in a fiduciary capacity. It helps provide a structured approach to meet to discuss charitable giving programs and grant-making strategies. Philanthropy can be a great point of entry into wealth discussions for the rising generation. Talking about giving to a nonprofit that reflects family values is easier than talking to the next generation about family values. Integrating philanthropy under the FTC can be an excellent way to pass on healthy attitudes about money and helping others.

These initiatives enable the family to make a positive impact on society while preserving its legacy of philanthropy. By centralizing control over philanthropic endeavors, the FTC streamlines the decision-making process and maximizes the effectiveness of charitable contributions while aligning the family around impactful giving.

Reduction of Family Conflicts

A structured governance framework formalizes decision-making structures and transparency standards. This framework fosters communication and collaboration among family members, striving to reduce the likelihood of conflicts arising from misunderstandings.

Family members are provided with a platform to participate in decision-making and understand their role as a beneficiary in addition to understanding the role of the Trustee. Transparency promotes unity and consensus around shared objectives, minimizing the potential for disputes that can erode family cohesion.

Education and Empowerment

An FTC can take on an educational role within the family. As family members are beneficiaries of the trusts managed by the FTC, the FTC may design and fund educational opportunities for family members. Educational programs and resources can be tailored to the unique needs of each generation, ensuring that beneficiaries are equipped to navigate the responsibilities of being a good steward. Education can also center on non-financial matters such as communication styles, health and wellbeing, technology and more—whatever topic is helpful to enhancing the family's capital beyond just financial capital.

Adaptation to Changing Circumstances

An FTC's flexibility is a strategic advantage in adapting to evolving family circumstances and its financial landscape. It can pivot to accommodate changing family priorities, financial goals, or unforeseen events. Whether addressing shifts in investment priorities, accommodating the entry of new family members, or responding to changing tax regulations, an FTC can proactively adjust its approach to align with the family's evolving needs. This agility is particularly valuable in the context of multigenerational wealth management, where long-term planning must account for a dynamic environment.

A Deeper Dive into FTCs

Family Case: XYZ, Inc.

Here is how an FTC works in the context of one family business.

In the early 1940s, Duncan Campbell started XYZ Inc., a concrete business in eastern Ohio. Duncan's three children were actively involved in the business, each working in various leadership capacities. With their "boots under the same table" each night, this second generation (G2) personally watched, lived, and understood the sacrifices required to make XYZ successful. At the dinner table, Duncan and his wife (G1) imparted their wisdom, as well as their vision and values, to their children. As G1 aged, they transferred ownership interest in XYZ outright to G2 in equal shares.

Fast forward to today, G2 has grown XYZ from a small, local business to a regional leader in the industry. XYZ is a successful and highly profitable company with some grandchildren (G3) actively involved at different levels of management. Two spouses are also working at the company. However, not all G3 family members want to join XYZ and have chosen different career paths. The family is wealthy, growing, and geographically dispersed, thus no longer do they have "boots under the same table" each night. Now it's different families with different parental influences including spousal influence bringing a completely different family perspective.

G2 is ready to retire, plus their advisors are encouraging them to complete estate plans, given the continued appreciation of XYZ shares. G2 recognizes the risk of XYZ shares being included in the estates of individual family members. Their primary concern is that an untimely death—or worse, multiple untimely deaths—could put pressure on XYZ to help meet the estate tax obligation of individual family members who own a highly valuable but illiquid asset within their estate with insufficient liquidity to cover estate tax obligations.

The family anticipates that the executor of a family member's estate would turn to XYZ to assist in creating liquidity to meet the tax obligation by redeeming shares from the estate. In addition, G2 realizes that as each generation creates trusts, selecting different trustees, current and successor trustees would multiply. These trustees would potentially be more removed from the family and particularly from the family's mission, vision, and values.

Further, the trustees' lack of knowledge about XYZ could lead to distractions when the company's managers are called to educate numerous trustees on XYZ's strategy. More importantly, XYZ's managers would feel the need to justify the reason the shares should remain in trusts, even as a concentrated position. That's because trustees are under a legal duty to diversify assets held in a trust. So, they frequently want to liquidate concentrated positions, such as ownership shares in a single business. Finally, the larger the family becomes, G2 worries that the family's values, traditions, and overall commitment to the family and XYZ are being weakened.

Over time, the family has worked to keep family stories and the history of XYZ alive through regular family gatherings designed to provide updates on the company's progress as well as to foster positive family relationships. Harmonious family decisions can be facilitated by generational groups knowing each other and having the time to build trust. Although it's clear that the family meetings are helpful and important, G2 also realizes a more formal structure is needed for these events to continue. They also want to expand family activities, such as family trips and retreats, to keep the clan connected.

Lastly, many G3 family members have expressed an interest in continuing to be a part of XYZ and few have a desire to divest of their grandfather's legacy. How can this legacy be supported across generations with some G3 family members working in the company and others not?

Can the family do anything different to avoid these problems:

- A proliferation of trustees who are not well versed in the business and are disconnected from the family's heritage and values

- The prospect of ever-increasing fragmentation of company ownership in each successive generation

- The growing risk of family disharmony because of geographic dispersal, spousal influence and family members' lack of interest in the business enterprise

Enter the FTC. It allows a family to remain involved in, and maintain control over, the family business as shareholders while also preparing for the future of both family members and the family business. The formation of an FTC can help families achieve this delicate balance between the present and future by providing a flexible and adaptable structure allowing family participation on the FTC's Board of Directors and/or committees. This flexibility permits individual family members to decide whether they want to remain actively involved in shareholder decisions in the family business or to choose passive involvement while having an economic benefit in the business. And, moreover, it can do so while insulating family advisors and family members from personal fiduciary liability.

Retaining control over the family business through an FTC being trustee of family trusts also benefits families interested in keeping the family business privately held across generations. Establishing a Family Business Asset Committee can focus shareholder decisions in a subset of the family and its advisors best situated to make well-considered shareholder decisions. An FTC can provide educational opportunities for all family members, including the rising generation, and can offer engagement opportunities for a wider number of family members regardless of whether they are actively involved in the operations of the family business.

While the family no longer has the benefit of "boots under the same table," it can create a sense of common purpose and intergenerational harmony, and in essence have "boots under the same roof."

Sources of Confusion about FTCs

When I give presentations to advisors and attorneys, questions always arise about three topics in particular: "Who is the trustee?", "How does the FTC manage business succession planning?", and "How is an FTC different from a family office?" I'd like to address them here.

Who is the Trustee?

Unlike the conventional arrangement with an individual trustee, the FTC itself functions as the trustee. This means that the decision-making authority isn't vested in a single person or a third-party institution—there is no "individual" trustee. Instead, it lies within the purview of the FTC, which is actually a corporate trustee, but a unique one that is owned and controlled by the family. Within the FTC, decisions are typically made at the Board and Committee level. The FTC Officers are frequently responsible for assisting in the implementation of the decisions and strategies. Therefore, there is not one single individual that makes all of the decisions related to the family trusts. The FTC *is* the trustee.

In essence, an FTC operates like an institutional corporate trustee but with a significant difference: the decision-makers are family members themselves, except for some specific decisions such as distribution decisions, which must be made by an independent person. These decisions can be further compartmentalized through committees, allowing for confidentiality within the decision-making structure. For instance, if a family member requires private medical treatment, the distribution committee can make decisions while keeping the specifics confidential from the broader board and family.

Who Manages the Business's Succession Plans?

It's important to note that the FTC is not involved in the day-to-day operations of a family business or the oversight of leadership succession planning for the family-owned enterprise, also called Business Succession Planning (BSP), as previously noted. As distinguished above, succession planning primarily focuses on identifying and mentoring future leaders within the business, ensuring a smooth transition of management. How these decisions are made doesn't change. If there is a Board of the family business, that Board remains responsible for the oversight of the family business' operations. The FTC's central purpose, on the other hand, revolves around managing the Shareholder Transition Planning (STP). (Please see my detailed discussion about BSP vs STP in Chapter 1.)

In essence, an FTC operates as a unique family-driven institution responsible for managing the ownership aspects of a family-owned business. While closely related to BSP, its primary focus is supporting the transfer of the beneficial ownership of the family business to future generations. BSP focuses on the business and STP focuses more on the family.

How is an FTC Different from a Family Office?

It is important to distinguish an FTC from a family office. Both an FTC and a family office can provide services such as tax, accounting, financial, legal and investment services, among others to a single family (family offices can also serve multiple families). Beyond offering various support services to family members, an FTC also has fiduciary powers to act as trustee of family trusts and must be established in a state that has specific statutes that authorize FTCs. The family office does not have fiduciary powers and can be set up in any state. In short, a family office is not an FTC, but an FTC may also operate as a family office.

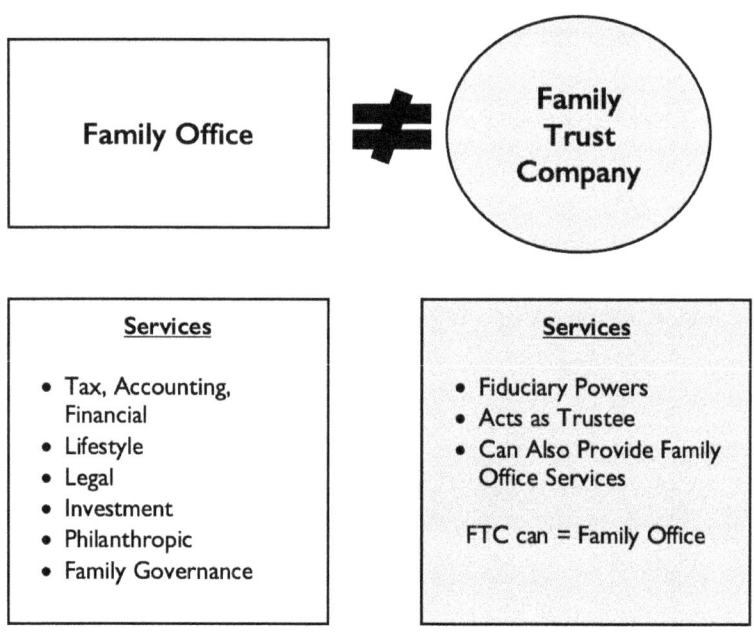

CHAPTER 4

Benefits of FTCs

Navigating the intricate landscape of family wealth management can be a daunting task, particularly when it involves preserving financial legacies for future generations. FTCs can be a part of a powerful planning strategy. I will highlight the many advantages provided by FTCs in the context of one family.

Family Case: The Garcias

We will follow the Garcia family, owners of a commercial estate company, to illustrate how these benefits come to life in real-world scenarios.

A Seat at the Table

In traditional trust arrangements, beneficiaries often feel like passive recipients of wealth, leading to misunderstandings and strained family dynamics. However, in an FTC, beneficiaries are encouraged to be involved in various decision-making opportunities. With their FTC in place, the Garcia children are on the Board that regularly meets to discuss stewardship of the family assets as trustee. They each serve on a committee aligned with their personal interests, such as the investment or education committee. This engagement not only ensures transparency but also avoids conflicts that can arise when beneficiaries feel excluded. Working together in the FTC also provides opportunities for them to build trust among each other as they meet regularly with the opportunity for open dialogue.

Shareholder Transition Planning

The Garcias use their FTC to plan for the next generation's involvement. The FTC helps facilitate the smooth transfer of ownership to the younger members of the family. By setting up trusts, they have gradually transferred beneficial ownership of the shares over time, allowing the children to learn about the business without the burden of direct ownership. This structured approach ensured that the business continued to thrive as it passed to the next generation.

Family Control

With a majority of the FTC Board comprised of family members, the Garcias make key decisions about the FTC's investments and shareholder matters such as electing directors of the business board. Moreover, the Garcias established committees with family advisors and trusted individuals who understand the family's history and long-term vision.

Estate Tax Mitigation

The family utilizes their FTC to act as trustee for smart estate tax strategies such as establishing Dynasty Trusts to hold ownership of the family business. By developing a gifting plan of moving shares into trusts that utilizes valuation discounts such as lack of marketability and control for a family business, they significantly reduced their estate tax liabilities, ensuring more of their wealth stays within the family for generations to come.

Trust Administration

Managing multiple family trusts can be complex, but not for the Garcias. Their FTC streamlines trust administration, ensuring continuity and transparency. Plus, by pooling resources across family trusts, they reduce trustee costs. Since their FTC doesn't have a large profit motive, they can prioritize the family's best interests and maintain limited liability for family members and trusted advisors serving in the FTC.

Trustee Succession

With the help of trusted advisors, the Garcias have a well-thought-out trustee succession plan, ensuring oversight of family member trusts over time. As the FTC acts as the perpetual trustee, they've standardized the family's trustee succession plan across individual family member trusts. This approach guarantees the ongoing stewardship of family wealth and assets by both family and trusted advisors.

Privacy and Confidentiality

Protecting their financial affairs and asset details is a top priority for the family. Their FTC shields their family's privacy, steering clear of public probate proceedings by ensuring family members place ownership of the family business in trusts. Unlicensed (or unregulated) FTCs like theirs aren't subject to state-government oversight or audits by banking regulators, ensuring a confidential and secure environment for managing sensitive information.

Institutionalized Fiduciary Management

The Garcias understand that removing administrative burdens from individual family members serving as trustees is vital. Their FTC does just that, allowing family members to focus on other priorities. Formal policies and procedures standardize the beneficiary experience, ensure proper documentation of fiduciary decisions, and protect the integrity of trust planning. By getting comfortable with giving up "dominion and control" of the family ownership, since they trust that the FTC is aligned with their vision, grantors like the Garcias avoid potential estate-tax complications.

Safeguarding Family Values

For the Garcias, integrating their family's values into the trustee/beneficiary relationship is essential. Their FTC's wealth strategies align with the family's core principles, including facilitating philanthropic endeavors that reflect their charitable goals. This ensures that their wealth is used not just wisely, but also in a way that reflects their deeply-held values.

Increasing Transparency

The Garcias have established formal governance structures within their FTC, fostering communication and collaboration among family members. This proactive approach encourages transparency around trust structures and promotes unity and consensus around shared objectives, ultimately having the potential to reduce conflicts that can arise from misunderstandings or disputes.

Facilitating Multi-Generational Involvement

With their FTC, the Garcias actively engage the rising generations in wealth management. They provide educational opportunities for financial responsibilities, knowledge about the family business and introduce trusted advisors across generations, ensuring continuity and the preservation of institutional knowledge. Long-term advisors can be introduced to the next generation to assist in ensuring continuity across generations. New advisors can have a seat at the table to learn about the senior generation's values and intentions for the trusts they have created ensuring continuity across generations.

Flexibility with Wealth Strategies

The Garcias value the flexibility that their FTC offers. It allows them to customize investment strategies, adapt to changing economic conditions, continue family beneficial ownership of the family business, and accommodate evolving family needs. With varying perspectives on the family and its wealth, their FTC ensures that everyone's input can be considered, offering opportunities for alternative investing options and maintaining closely held assets.

As you can see, FTCs offer an array of advantages, ensuring the smooth transition of assets across generations, reducing estate tax liabilities, and safeguarding family values. FTCs can bring clarity to governance structures and encourage multigenerational involvement. Like for the Garcia family, FTCs can become guardians of family legacies, promoting unity and continuity across generations.

CHAPTER 5

FTC Structures: An Overview

As I previously noted, an FTC is a family-owned and family-controlled entity, but within this seemingly simple definition lies a multifaceted organizational structure that is designed to meet the objectives of a specific family. It encompasses a range of directors, officers, committees, policies and procedures which are all carefully designed to facilitate the management and preservation of family assets, family business, and the realization of the family's goals.

I want to describe the structure of a typical FTC and offer details about how this flexible framework enables families to navigate the complexities of multigenerational wealth based on their own vision. Each family decides which committees to utilize and how to involve family members. At the very basic structure, an FTC has an Investment Committee, Discretionary Distribution Committee, and an Amendment Committee. Other committees, as demonstrated by the below chart, can be employed, or not, depending on the particular goals of a family.

Family Trust Company
(an Ohio corporation)

Officers
Chairman (optional)
President
Secretary
Assistant Secretary
Treasurer
Assistant Treasurer

- The FTC serves as the Trustee of Family Trusts supported by the FTC Officers & Committees
- The FTC has a written Code of Regulations addressing the responsibilities of the Board of Directors, Officers, and Committees
- The FTC has a written Policy & Procedure manual setting forth operational guidance

Investment Committee
Makes decisions with respect to the investment of the non-Family Business Asset

Works with Investment Managers and Investment Advisors

Discretionary Distribution Committee (DDC)
Makes decisions with respect to discretionary distributions to beneficiaries

Comprised of Independent Persons

Family Business Asset Committee
Responsible for making shareholder decisions related to Family Business Asset

(Sometimes not "activated" until voting shares are in trust under management of FTC)

Education Committee
Determines and oversees educational programming for beneficiaries

Philanthropy Committee
Determines & coordinates the family's philanthropic giving

(Can be informal family meetings)

Amendment Committee
Only convenes in limited circumstances to address changes to tax-sensitive powers in governing documents

Engagement Committee
Develops "family glue" activities to keep the family connected & informed of family milestone events (reunions, newsletters, rising-generation activities, etc.)

How an FTC Functions

Trustee of the Family Trusts

An FTC acts as the trustee for various family trusts, each created to serve specific purposes and beneficiaries. These trusts can include individual revocable trusts, dynasty trusts, and specialized trusts like Irrevocable Life Insurance Trusts (ILITs) and Annual

Exclusion Gifting Trusts. The FTC ensures these trusts are managed in accordance with their terms to ensure compliance with proper trust administration.

FTC Governing Documents

As a company, the FTC has its own governing documents that serve as the foundation for the organization's governance structure and operational guidelines. Below are some key components addressed within the FTC's governing documents:

- **Board Composition:** Defines the composition of the Board of Directors, specifying the number of family and non-family members who serve as Directors. This section may also detail the qualifications, responsibilities, and term limits of board members. For instance, it might stipulate that Family Directors must have a trust under the management of the FTC to serve on the Board—thus ensuring the Family Director has "skin in the game." Characteristics and requirements to serve as an Independent Director can be memorialized such as age requirements, professional licenses, or length of time serving multigenerational families, to name a few. These characteristics are as distinct as each family, but always reflective of the family's values.

- **Committee Charters:** Provides guidance on the establishment and roles of various committees within the FTC. Committees play a crucial role in addressing specific aspects of the FTC's operations and are where family members may have an interest in lending their particular human capital. Family members previously not engaged in the family enterprise may find their 'niche' serving on an FTC committee. This section may include details on committee charters, their composition, and their responsibilities.

- **Decision-Making Processes:** Outlines the decision-making processes within the FTC such as by majority, super-majority or unanimous decisions. One client selected unanimous decision making to ensure the "family kept talking" when there were areas of disagreement—this may not work for all families, but was the preference for this family. This section may include details on voting procedures, quorum requirements, and dispute resolution mechanisms.

- **Accountability and Reporting:** Establishes mechanisms for accountability and reporting within the FTC. It may require regular reporting to the Board, detailing the FTC's financial performance, trust administration activities, and other relevant matters. It may also specify that certain authority for decisions is delegated to a committee with no need for the decisions to be ratified by the Board, thus ensuring confidentiality where desired by the family.

- **Amendment Procedures:** Addresses how amendments to the FTC's governing documents can be made. A formal process is required for approving changes to the FTC's governing documents, ensuring that any modifications align with the overall family's evolving needs and objectives.

Policy and Procedure Manual

The Policy and Procedure Manual (PPM) is an essential document that provides detailed operational guidance for the organization's day-to-day activities ensuring the FTC operates under fiduciary best practices. The PPM serves as a crucial resource ensuring that the FTC's decisions are properly documented. Here are some examples:

- An investment policy outlines the FTC's approach to managing the assets held within family trusts reflecting the family's investment philosophy. It provides a comprehensive framework for investment decisions, including asset allocation strategies, risk tolerance guidelines, and diversification strategies (or direction not to diversify family business assets).

- Discretionary distributions from family trusts are a significant aspect of the FTC's responsibilities. The PPM includes a policy and procedure for discretionary distributions providing a structured approach to requesting a distribution and information to be reviewed by the Discretionary Distribution Committee in making distribution decisions.

Governance

At the FTC's helm are the Board of Directors with the assistance of the Officers. The core leadership of an FTC are the Officers, which typically include, at minimum, a president, treasurer, and secretary. Together, they work to implement the decisions of the Board and committees of the FTC, or oversee an outsourced provider handling day-to-day operations.

The president's responsibilities include serving as the FTC's chief executive officer exercising supervision over the business activities of the FTC, including, but not limited to, the following:

- Supervision and responsibility for any personnel and operations in connection with the handling of trust accounts, including the keeping of appropriate records and systems

- Sign trust instruments and accept trusts on behalf of the FTC, provided that the President is not the grantor of such trust, in which case such authority will be delegated to another officer who is not the grantor of such trust

- Preside at all meetings of shareholders, and in the absence of a chairman of the Board, shall preside at all meetings of directors

- Provide general supervision over the administration of accounts including ensuring that mandatory distributions are timely distributed from trusts

- Oversee the submission of matters to the DDC, the Investment Committee or the Amendment Committee

The secretary is primarily responsible for maintaining accurate records and documentation. Responsibilities include:

- Provide proper meeting notices for shareholder and director meetings

- Keep minutes of all the proceedings of the shareholders and the Directors

- Maintain documentation associated with the Board and pertinent organizational documents

- Perform duties as the President may from time to time delegate

The treasurer's responsibilities include:

- Oversee the accounting, financial reporting and tax reporting functions of the FTC
- Create and maintain FTC's annual budget for each fiscal year including presenting the budget to the Board
- Provide financial reports at each meeting of the FTC Board of Directors
- Oversee trustee fee calculation and process payment
- Perform duties as the President may from time to time delegate

Committees

Committees play an important role within the FTC. Committees can serve diverse functions, from overseeing discretionary distributions and investments to promoting family engagement, education and philanthropy. Here, I'd like to offer some insight into how an FTC's committees can address some key topics.

Discretionary Distribution Committees

Discretionary Distribution Committees (DDCs) serve as the decision makers for discretionary distributions from the trusts under the FTC's management. Creatively, DDCs can be established for each family branch, by beneficiary, or even by a specific trust if the FTC's governing documents are drafted allowing this level of flexibility. Members of the DDC must be independent persons by IRS guidance. Therefore, family members typically do not serve on this committee.

DDCs are entrusted with the responsibility of determining the timing and amount of the distributions from a trust to a beneficiary.

Their primary objective is to consider the diverse needs and circumstances of beneficiaries, ensuring that distributions align with the grantor's intentions while addressing the unique situation of each beneficiary which can change over time and differ by beneficiary.

I encourage grantors I work with to take the time to create thoughtful grantor intention language to supplement the terms of the trust document. Although the thoughts and aspirations shared by the grantor aren't legally binding, it may become a precious document in the future for sharing why the grantor set up the trust and what the grantor's vision was for the utilization of the trust funds. Future beneficiaries can have a window into their ancestor's vision and values. More contemporarily, the grantor intention language can serve as a guide—or North Star—for the DDC when considering discretionary distribution requests.

In the best of circumstances, members of the DDC may become mentors to the beneficiaries it serves. For example, should a beneficiary want a distribution to create a business, the DDC could act as a sounding board for the business plan created by the beneficiary. DDC members may become another trusted individual within the beneficiary's sphere.

Given the decisions of the DDC can be very private and personal, the FTC's corporate documents can be drafted in a way that the DDC's decisions aren't ratified by the Board. Since the Board is comprised primarily of family members, this helps establish some boundaries for being "under the same roof" but acknowledging there are very personal requests that may be considered by the DDC.

Family Case: The Shapiro Family's DDCs

Consider the Shapiro family, a multigenerational family with diversified interests and financial needs but bound together by a family business started by Sam Shapiro many years ago, Shapiro, Inc. The success of Shapiro, Inc. has continued allowing family members to find fulfilling careers within the company, but also family members have branched out finding success outside of Shapiro, Inc. The Shapiro family's FTC has established separate DDCs for each of its three family branches, recognizing that each family branch may have distinct dynamics, perspectives, and financial situations.

Let's focus on one branch, that includes Sarah Shapiro, Sam's granddaughter and a trust beneficiary, who is herself an entrepreneur running a successful tech startup after listening to her grandfather's many stories from the early years of the business. Sarah and her children are beneficiaries of a trust set up by Sam years ago. Some of Sarah's children are actively involved in the family business established by Sarah's father, while others have pursued careers outside the family business. None of her children have joined her in her tech startup, but her children are also very entrepreneurial by nature. To support the branch's strong entrepreneurial spirit, the DDC is comprised of three members including an independent member with a strong business background including multiple startups along with two additional trusted advisors with a long history advising various members of the Shapiro family.

When a request for a discretionary distribution is brought before the DDC, it includes information about the trust and its assets based on a procedure outlined in the FTC's Policy & Procedure Manual. Members of the DDC consider factors such as the requesting beneficiary's financial goals, educational needs, and business venture potential, if applicable. They also assess the impact of the distribution on the long-term goals of the trust including consideration of assets available to other current and future beneficiaries. As part of the process, the terms of the trust are considered as well as grantor intention language written by Sam Shapiro when he first set up the trust.

In this case, Sarah's son, Adam, has requested a distribution from a trust to launch a company based on a promising technology innovation. Adam has submitted a detailed business plan outlining the project and the potential. The DDC reviews the proposal carefully and requests additional information from Adam to assist with their decision. They assess the potential of the project, but also consider having the trust invest in the business, thus the trust maintaining ownership, versus providing Adam with the distribution directly to provide him full control and ownership of the business. After rigorous deliberation and due diligence, the DDC considers the amount of the request and decides to make the distribution to Adam. As part of their decision process, the DDC thoughtfully considered this nonbinding intention language Sam Shapiro had written:

"I would support distributions to enable my lineal descendants to establish new businesses or ventures. I would hope that before such a distribution is made, the Trustee would assess the commitment, character, and preparedness of the Beneficiary making the request. In addition, I hope that the Trustee require a business plan with appropriate complexity for the size of the venture to ensure the business concept has been well researched and planned. My thought is that the Trustee may commit funds from the Trusts by way of loan, direct payment to the Beneficiary, stock purchase in the new business, etc., but keeping in mind the need to limit the exposure of any other assets of the Trusts to the risks of the business."

Investment Committees

The Investment Committee holds a crucial role with the responsibility of determining the investment strategies for liquid assets held in the trusts. Note that later in this section, I address the oversight of the family business asset ownership under a Family Business Asset Committee. Like the DDCs, multiple Investment Committees may be established in recognition of varying investment perspectives within the family. However, it is most common that there is one Investment Committee established with the responsibility to invest the liquid assets in all trusts under the management of the FTC which also strengthens the opportunity to leverage more assets to access a wider range of investment opportunities.

The primary responsibilities of the Investment Committees include:

- Overseeing the investment of liquid assets held within family trusts. This involves evaluating investment opportunities, diversifying portfolios, and making decisions aligned with the family's long-term wealth strategy.

- Developing investment policy statements to reflect the appropriate strategies for each trust and its associated beneficiaries balancing risk, return and short-term liquidity needs. Investment strategies are not static; they must adapt to changing market conditions, economic trends, and the family's evolving needs.

- Monitoring performance to closely track the performance of trust assets—frequently against benchmarks established by the Investment Committee when determining the family's overall investment philosophy. Quarterly reviews are common and annual assessments of the investment managers/advisors ensure that the FTC continues to work with professionals aligned with the family's expectations.

Families with limited expertise in overseeing liquid assets—frequent in family businesses that don't consider investing as being in their "wheelhouse"—can rely on the support of independent expertise through having independent members on the committee. However, an Investment Committee can also be an opportunity for family members with appropriate expertise to contribute to the family enterprise and become more engaged with the FTC. In addition, the Investment Committee can make the decision to delegate investment authority to an investment manager versus keeping the sole responsibility for making investment decisions within the FTC. If investment discretion is delegated to an investment manager, the Investment Committee is then responsible for monitoring the performance of the investment manager and annually completing due diligence to ensure it is prudent to continue with the relationship.

Having an independent member with investment expertise on the Investment Committee can be beneficial for multiple reasons. Here's why their participation can be important:

- One of the key benefits is the educational opportunity for family members on the committee to learn from the independent member. This opportunity may be just the factor that engages a family member.

- Independent members bring diverse perspectives to the committee. This diversity of thought can be invaluable in crafting well-rounded investment strategies that consider various risk factors and market conditions.

- As outsiders to the family, independent members can offer objective insights into investment decisions. They are less likely to be influenced by familial biases or dynamics, ensuring that investment choices are driven by sound financial principles.

- In cases where family members have differing opinions on investment strategies, the independent member can help to provide education and perspectives that the family members may not have experienced.

Family Case: Anderson Family Investment Committees

The Anderson family, spanning multiple generations, established an FTC to manage the family trusts which hold their substantial wealth, including multiple businesses, real estate holdings, and liquid assets. Considering the different holdings in family trusts and varying investment philosophies, the FTC has an Investment Committee for each family branch, and each committee includes at least one independent member, depending on the investment expertise within the family branch.

In this scenario, Jane, an investment professional with a background in portfolio management, serves as the independent member on the Investment Committee for the eldest branch of the Anderson family. Jane was selected because her penchant for carefully selecting investments and holding them for the long run aligned with the family branch's investment philosophy. This was an area Jane was well-seasoned in given her over 20 years of experience investing. Her role is to provide unbiased insights, challenge conventional thinking when necessary, and help the committee make well-informed investment decisions.

Recently, the committee was faced with significant market volatility. While some family members were anxious and wanted to sell, others were willing to hold the portfolio and ride out the ups and downs. Jane played a vital role in keeping the family members on course without impulsive action. Her insights and steadfast experience allowed the committee to hold firm with their investment strategy.

Amendment Committee

The Amendment Committee is tasked with reviewing and approving proposed amendments to the FTC's governing documents that change any "tax-sensitive" powers. This is a technical committee comprised of independent persons. This committee typically isn't required to meet as if governing documents are initially properly drafted, changes aren't frequently made to "tax-sensitive" powers. However, this highlights the need to work with an advisor familiar with setting up FTCs to ensure the proper IRS guidance is followed.

Family Business Asset Committee

The Family Business Asset Committee plays an important shareholder role when the family's wealth includes a family-owned business held in family trusts. This committee is dedicated to the shareholder oversight of the family business as well as voting any shareholder decisions for ownership of the family business held in the trusts under the management of the FTC. Establishing a Family Business Asset Committee provides a means to limit the oversight of the family business to a smaller group of shareholders by limiting the membership on the Family Business Asset

Committee to family shareholders with the most appropriate expertise relative to the family business—or to trusted advisors bringing unique expertise. Even for a client with over 150 family trusts, all of the family-business ownership in those trusts can be overseen by the Family Business Asset Committee—frequently comprised of three to five members. Normally, there is a requirement that a majority of the committee's members have (or had) experience working in the family business to ensure that shareholder decisions are thoughtfully made by a well-educated group. Adding some independent members to the committee can also bring an outside perspective to shareholder decisions. Centralizing this decision making can be very beneficial versus the common problem of "herding cats" when, over the course of several generations, the number of direct owners can expand to a frustratingly unmanageable size without thoughtful estate planning. A Family Business Asset Committee consolidates the shareholder decision process with fewer shareholder questions being posed to company management and a highly educated group making shareholder decisions associated with the family's ownership of the company.

Engagement Committee

Some families choose to have an Engagement Committee, similar to what is sometimes known as a Family Council. It is dedicated to fostering unity, communication, and active participation among family members—who are also trust beneficiaries. Its initiatives are aimed at strengthening familial bonds and preserving the family's legacy for multiple generations. Sometimes called "family glue," activities for this group include:

Family Meetings

The committee arranges and coordinates regular family meetings or reunions. These gatherings provide opportunities for family members to come together, share experiences, and discuss various aspects of the family's business, philanthropic endeavors and just plain having fun together! Meetings can take various forms, from annual conferences to special events to quarterly conference-call updates, and they often serve as a platform for addressing important family decisions. Family gatherings are a great way to keep families together over time. Family members who know each other well and learn together may also work well together.

Educational Programs (sometimes coordinated by an Education Committee, if one is established)

To equip family members with the knowledge and skills important to the family, the committee organizes educational programs and workshops. These sessions can cover a wide range of topics, including financial literacy, estate planning, investment strategies, philanthropic endeavors, cybersecurity, wellness recommendations, communication strategies or any other topic of interest to the family. Educational programs ensure that family members are supported by the FTC structure not just from a financial perspective, but from a holistic perspective.

Communication

Effective communication is at the heart of family unity and cohesiveness. The Engagement Committee can develop and implement newsletters and dedicated family portals that keep family members informed about the FTC's initiatives. Newsletters can also be a great way for family members to share updates on important life events with pictures speaking a thousand words! This helps keep the family connected and up to date on family members' achievements or important happenings.

History

Every family business has a story to tell—important lessons about hard work, perseverance, leadership, innovation, and business philosophy. However, those valuable lessons are lost when founders and family elders pass away without taking the time to record their stories. The Engagement Committee can take on the responsibility for making sure history isn't lost.

Whether it's a commemorative book, documentary videos, or oral history recordings, a family history project can become a wonderful family glue activity that strengthens the bonds across family branches and through the generations. Plus, researchers at Emory University have shown that children show higher levels of emotional well-being if they know stories about relatives who came before them.[17]

Documenting family stories is good for the family's business, too. Articulating a family company's heritage, culture, and vision can not only help key stakeholders learn from its past but also improve the organization's bottom line. History projects can highlight their uniqueness and principles, fostering a sense of belonging among employees. In addition, marketing and sales efforts benefit from the insights gained through a deep understanding of the company's culture and value proposition.

More specifically, here are examples of family engagement activities:

- The Annual Family Retreat brings together multiple generations of the family. Retreats can be held at a vacation destination or special family place of significance and are frequently planned for the same week/weekend every year. The retreat can offer a mix of fun recreational activities, business updates, philanthropy projects and educational sessions. It provides a relaxed setting for family members to reconnect, discuss the family business or wealth strategies, and nurture bonds. Cousins that grow up spending time together help facilitate the family staying together over time because they get to know—and hopefully like—their extended family. From learning to play together they learn to work together—in the family business or as part of the family enterprise including the FTC.

- Education Programming can be offered in many different ways. Some families conduct educational programming once a year at the Annual Family Retreat. Others offer programming quarterly through video conference calls. Even others record podcasts that are available to family members to listen to at their convenience. The important concept is that the committee is meeting the educational needs of the family members.

- There are numerous conferences available for families to attend to network with similarly situated families which offers an opportunity to "normalize" some of the similar issues facing families as well as learn various approaches other families have employed when tackling challenges. These conferences offer a unique opportunity for family members to engage in open discussions about their roles in preserving the family's heritage and wealth with different families. Conference attendance can be supported by the FTC budget and family members can return to share the knowledge they gained at the conference.

The Engagement Committee can plan all these activities for family members with a budget supported by the FTC since the family members are typically also the trust beneficiaries of the family trusts.

An FTC can also have other committees that, over time, become essential components of effective governance and decision-making for the family. They contribute to the family by addressing aspects that arise over time for the family such as education, philanthropy, and governance continuity. Here are some additional examples:

Education Committee

An Education Committee is dedicated to empowering family members with the knowledge and skills necessary to navigate topics of interest to the trust beneficiaries. Its role can promote financial literacy or any topic that is important to the family. How and when to tell children about wealth, challenges of social media, risk management, effective communication styles, addressing conflict, prenuptial agreements, estate planning, physical wellbeing, and many more are topics that can be tackled through programming developed by the Education Committee!

Family Case: The Marino Family Education Committee

The Marino family, spanning four generations, recognized the importance of educating family members. They established an Education Committee within their FTC. In one instance, the Education Committee organized a communication workshop for the rising generation. Each family member (lineal descendants and spouses) took the Myers–Briggs assessment. They then were offered individual debrief sessions to learn more about their leadership and communication styles. Many of the couples elected to have the debrief session done together, which provided very personal, and powerful, household-level communication perspectives. However, the most impactful component of this education was a Myers–Briggs "map" overlaying the styles of the family members in one generation. They learned how they might communicate as a group and tendencies they needed to guard against as the generation transitioned into the leaders of the family. It reinforced their understanding of how to work together as a generation in decision making while respecting the styles of their cousins that were different.

Philanthropy Committee

A Philanthropy Committee can be involved in guiding the family's charitable endeavors and bringing the family to consensus on giving to do more impactful giving. This committee can provide the platform and space for the family members to identify charitable causes and organizations that resonate with the family's core values and beliefs. This alignment ensures that philanthropic efforts reflect the family's commitment to making a meaningful impact on the community and society at large. Further, to promote a culture of philanthropy within the family, the committee may organize volunteer initiatives for the entire family to participate in during a family meeting. These programs help family members understand the importance of giving back not only their treasure (money), but of their time and talent which is equally as important. In addition, volunteering sets an example for even the youngest family members when activities involving the youngsters are planned. Philanthropy is often considered to be one of the best introductions to family values as the family selects initiatives to support.

Family Case: The Weber Family Philanthropy Committee

The Weber family is known for their commitment to social responsibility—it's an important family value to give back. Their FTC's Philanthropy Committee began by conducting a family-wide survey to understand each member's charitable interests and values. Family members were provided with a list of charitable opportunities and a wide way to support their areas of interest—then were asked to vote on their top areas of interest. With this anonymous data, the family discovered a shared passion for education and decided to focus their joint charitable efforts on improving access to quality education in the communities where they had physical locations or the family business.

Over the years, the committee established partnerships with local schools and educational organizations. They provided funding for scholarships, after-school programs, and infrastructure improvements. These strategic initiatives not only aligned with the family's values but also created a lasting legacy of educational support in the communities where employees of the family business live and work.

CHAPTER 6

FTC Structures: Case Studies

Now that I have laid the foundation of what and how an FTC can become an integral component of a family's wealth strategy, I thought it would be helpful to share some real-life case studies of families that have set up an FTC. To protect the identity of families, some of the details have been changed. Each case study identifies the motivating factor(s) for setting up the FTC as well as unique structures that reflect the particular family's goals.

Family Case Study #1
G2 Thinking Like a G1 Wealth Creator

Motivation for setting up the FTC: Preparing children for future beneficial ownership of the family business and providing stewardship education

During his earlier years, Ned, a G2 family member had the unfortunate, negative experience involving a family dispute that necessitated he buyout his sibling's stake in the family business. His father had created the business, and Ned had worked in it his entire life. However, his sibling had not worked in the business nor had the sibling developed a long-term commitment to keeping the family business. Because of this difficult scenario, Ned developed a heightened awareness of the need for proactive intentional planning to avoid similar conflicts among his children as well as future generations—leading him to think much like a G1. His primary objectives were to consolidate ownership of the family business for future generations and instill a sense of stewardship among family members, transitioning from direct ownership to a trustee/beneficiary model of beneficial ownership. Ultimately, Ned also wanted to protect his children from the conflict he experienced with his sibling. Notably, none of Ned's children work in the family business.

One of the main challenges Ned faced was not uncommon for many successful businesses. In recent years the business had experienced substantial growth, making it financially challenging for the next generation to buy out non-participating family members without hampering the company's potential for growth. After researching various transition options, Ned settled on creating a Dynasty Trust with an unlicensed Ohio FTC as trustee. The FTC's Board, which meets twice a year, was comprised of Ned (the grantor) and his children (the beneficiaries of the Dynasty Trust) along with two trusted advisors. Notably, Ned's spouse was not included on the Board due to her history of keeping her distance from ownership of the business. As a result, the FTC's governing documents were drafted with the criteria that spouses are not eligible to serve on the Board, but can serve on Committees. This reflects the current family culture and values. The FTC started with only one trust under its management, but with a broader plan of adding trusts over time, plus the FTC was named as the successor trustee in the grantor's revocable documents. At his passing, a significant ownership stake of the family business will be held in a trust under the FTC's management. Most immediately, Ned's goal was to familiarize his family with the trustee function and provide transparency into how his estate plan will flow at his passing.

Three committees were set up:

- An Investment Committee consisting of Ned, his wife and his children, as well as one trusted advisor with investment expertise. Currently, this committee's role is limited due to the presence of only one trust within the FTC that frequently annually distributes dividends received from the family business to the trust beneficiaries. However, the structure is in place to step in when the situation changes.

- A Discretionary Distribution Committee comprising two Independent Directors. This committee makes decisions regarding the distribution of dividends from the family business that flow into the trust. Following best practice, the committee keeps clear meeting minutes regarding the distribution decisions made.

- An Amendment Committee is tasked with approving changes to the FTC's governing documents affecting tax-sensitive powers. This committee must be comprised of independent persons and since it is not anticipated to be required to meet, the members are defined as the then-serving Independent Directors.

Notably, Ned's story demonstrates how an FTC can evolve over time as the needs of the family and trusts under management increase. However, in the meantime, this simple FTC structure is providing the educational opportunities and family engagement Ned desires for his children to prepare to be good stewards as the future beneficial owners of the family business upon his passing. Below is an outline of this FTC structure:

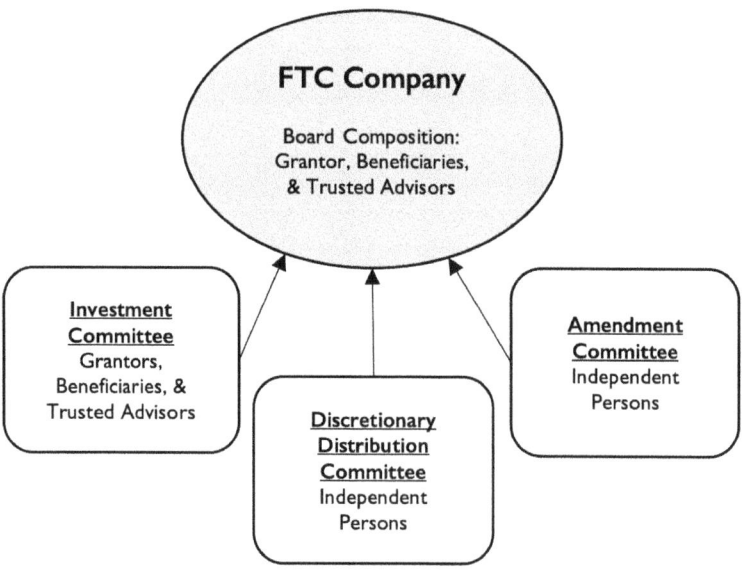

Family Case Study #2
Visionary G2 Siblings

Motivation for setting up the FTC: Control over the family business and minimizing estate taxes

A close-knit group of G2 siblings had a secure and thriving family business. Like most successful business owners, they focused much of their attention on the day-to-day operations of the company. They occasionally did long-term planning, but they never considered the possibility of any estate tax issues coming into play as the business grew. That was until their CPA ran projections showing significant growth of the company over the next three to five years—based on the company's actual growth historically. Seeing the numbers in black and white, the siblings soon recognized the impending estate tax challenges that could affect the family's financial legacy in just a few years should a sibling pass unexpectedly. With the voting shares firmly in their hands, they acknowledged the need to take immediate action to preserve their family's control over the family business and ensure its long-term viability.

With no estate planning done yet, the G2 siblings started with a blank slate based on their ownership of all the voting shares, as well as the nonvoting shares, of the family manufacturing company. Launching from G2s' concern regarding the shareholder decision-making process if all the voting shares were to be dispersed amongst G3 family members, a small Task Force of family members and trusted advisors began the process of exploring options to keep the voting shares consolidated as well as addressing the estate tax concerns. They realized it was difficult at times for all G2 family members to come to consensus and they were concerned that this process would become even more difficult if the voting shares were held by an even larger, more diverse group of family members. As the Task Force learned more about estate planning, they came to understand Dynasty Trusts and FTCs. Ultimately, the Task Force's recommendation was for the family to create an Ohio unlicensed FTC to act as trustee of family trusts that would hold all the voting stock of the family business plus a significant portion of the nonvoting stock.

G2, being very aligned in their desire for the company to continue across multiple generations, also decided to create one trust to hold *ALL* the voting stock ensuring that decision-making power remained centralized and overseen by a group with the necessary expertise to guide the shareholder decisions. Each G2 would also create an individual Dynasty Trust to be funded by nonvoting shares to ensure estate tax liabilities were minimized. This structure allowed for the orderly transition of nonvoting shares to the G3 generation over time. This family also wanted to consolidate control over the voting stock to a smaller group of individuals. Therefore, in a very creative design, this unlicensed Ohio FTC was set up with two Boards—the Family Asset Board and the General Board. The FTC was structured to specifically address their goals. The family instituted a quarterly meeting schedule, bringing together family members and FTC board members to strengthen family bonds and facilitate essential discussions about the family's vision for their legacy.

The FTC's committees were then established to meet the needs of both G3 and G4—beneficiaries of the family trusts. They established a Discretionary Distribution Committee, an Investment Committee, an Amendment Committee and an Engagement Committee.

The Family Asset Board is comprised of a majority of Independent Directors bringing expertise and an unbiased perspective to shareholder decisions as this group has the exclusive authority over the trust holding the voting stock. The Family Asset Board of Directors were named initially in the governing documents and are self-perpetuating. Nonvoting stock in the individual Dynasty Trusts are overseen by a General Board comprised of Family Branch Directors and two Independent Directors. The FTC's governing documents permit spouses to serve on the Board, but also encourages multi-generational and diverse representation of the family by its Family Branch Directors. The General Board, which meets four times a year, has the responsibility to oversee general governance, trust administration and compliance matters of the FTC.

Another unique feature of this FTC is its Engagement Committee, which is very active in conducting activities designed to keep the family engaged and informed. The committee's events are approved by the Family Asset Board and funded by dividends issued to voting shares. Since the trust holding the voting shares is held for the benefit of all lineal descendants and their spouses, it is aligned with the intentions of the entire family—remember, every G2 family member is a grantor of the voting trust having contributed their voting shares.

With the rising generation now facing college expenses, the Discretionary Distribution Committee member (this DDC only has one member) proactively designed a tuition payment policy he intends to follow when

FTC Structures: Case Studies

receiving discretionary distributions requests from the rising generation for tuition support. This proactive approach has provided parents with some certainty and ability to plan savings for their portion of covering higher education payments.

The next two diagrams outline this creative and unique structure that was designed to meet the vision of the family. This is truly an example of how an FTC can be flexible and customized to meet the family where it is and address various concerns.

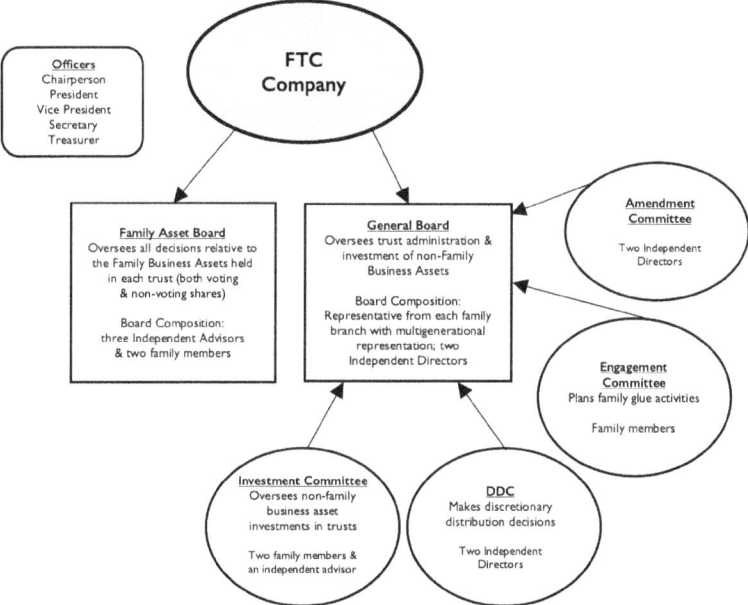

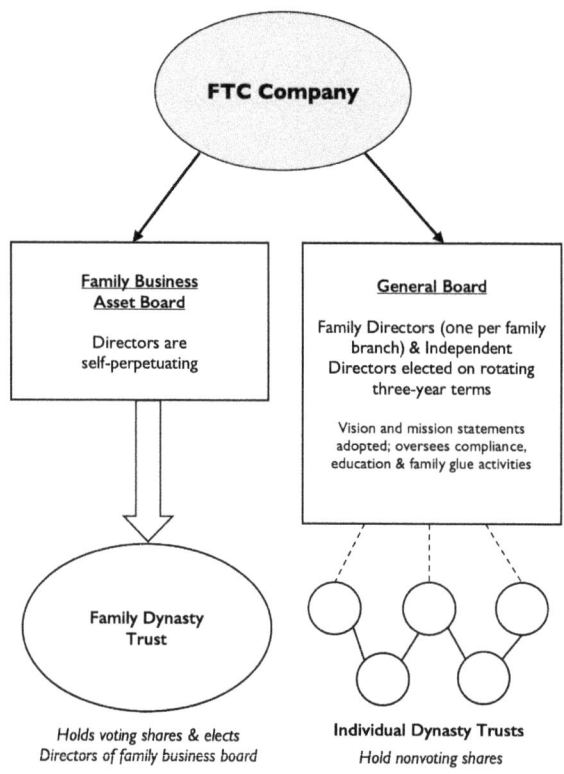

Family Case Study #3
Here Comes the Cousin Consortium

Motivation for setting up the FTC: Control of the family wealth strategy over LOTS of trusts with trustee succession issues

By the time a family matures to the third generation, it is sometimes called the cousin consortium as wealth flows to the next generation of family members beyond the siblings. How siblings may have been comfortable overseeing the family wealth may not be the same way cousins—who don't know each other as well and are geographically dispersed with differing financial situations—are comfortable managing the family wealth. Also, by the third generation, it is not uncommon for there to be numerous trusts holding the family wealth, with most family-business ownership based on beneficial ownership in trusts instead of outright, direct ownership.

This family has a significant number of legacy trusts. Before setting up an Ohio unlicensed FTC, the siblings were acting as individual trustees of each other's legacy trusts. They were comfortable serving in this role, which includes determining the trust's investment strategy and approving any discretionary distributions to beneficiaries. There are few G2s and they are close, having worked together for years. However, the rising generation of G3 cousins are numerous and not as familiar with their cousin counter parts as the sibling group is with each other. As written in the trust documents, the G3 cousins are next in line to serve as trustees of other cousins' trusts. This didn't sit well with the cousins overall. Although the concept of setting up an FTC had been contemplated by the G2 siblings, the FTC wasn't launched because the siblings were comfortable with "how things operated." With the transition to G3s on the horizon, it was time to re-consider setting up an FTC.

Another driving motivator was the diverging investment interests of the family. Although they continued to invest together on certain projects, they also had invested trust assets separately. The family readily saw the advantages of setting up one FTC, but they also wanted to continue segregating different trust investments.

With all of this nuances in mind, the structure of the FTC designed to meet the needs of this family features the following:

Board of Directors

The FTC holds regular meetings, gathering family members and FTC Board members together twice a year to discuss essential matters concerning wealth management and family governance. The Board is comprised of Family Directors and two Independent Directors. Initially, the

G2 siblings are the Family Directors. Over time, they intend to move the Family Directors to G3 family members.

Discretionary Distribution Committees

Due to privacy concerns and differing preferences among family branches, multiple DDCs were formed. These DDCs are responsible for making discretionary distribution decisions for the individual branches, thus respecting confidentiality and privacy since the decisions of the DDC are not ratified by the Board.

Investment Committee

The Investment Committee was established to oversee joint investments of non-family business assets held within the various trusts. It allowed the family together to explore opportunities in alternative investments, ensuring that their wealth was optimally managed and leveraging a larger pool of liquidity.

Family Business Asset Committees

As mentioned above, given the varying investments in family businesses, multiple Family Business Asset Committees were created to align investment strategies with each branch's preferences. This structure allowed for separate investment decisions within family branches while maintaining collaboration on joint investments, including jointly owned family business assets.

This case exemplifies how an FTC can provide effective solutions to complex family wealth and governance challenges, ensuring the preservation of both assets and family unity across generations.

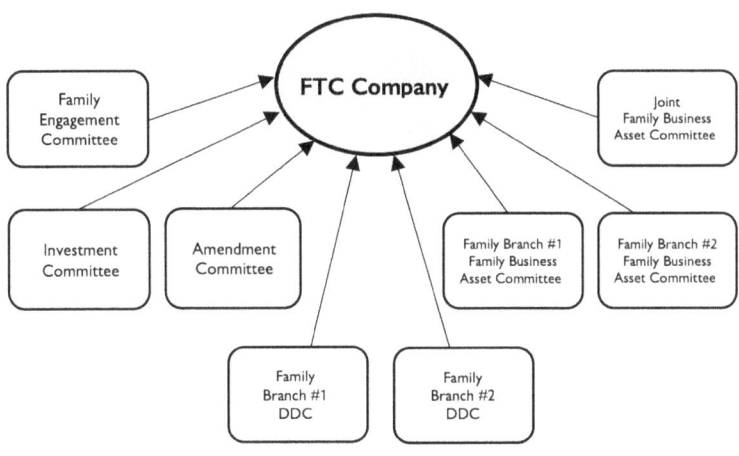

Family Case Study #4
G1 and His Spouse Sit at the Table with G2

Motivation for setting up the FTC: Promoting Transparency, Education, and Multigenerational Involvement

This case study revolves around George, a wealth creator who initiated the formation of an FTC driven by his realization that his children didn't understand the wealth strategy and role the family business plays in it. He had two main concerns. First, he wanted to ensure that his children knew the complexities of estate planning as well as the thoughtful planning that had already been done with significant ownership of the family business now in trusts; and second, he hoped the FTC would facilitate a harmonious transition between trusted advisors across generations.

An FTC was established with these features:

- Its Board convenes four times annually to keep the family engaged in regular dialogue with educational programming planned for every meeting.

- To foster transparency, education, and multigenerational involvement, George, his wife, and their two children serve on the FTC Board and committees. There are also two Independent Directors on the Board—one Independent Director is a long-time advisor to George. The other Independent Director was interviewed and selected as a new advisor—younger and closer to G2's age. George's thought process for bringing in a new advisor was to ensure the new Independent Director would have the opportunity to "sit at the table" with him and his wife to understand first hand their values and intentions for the family wealth. Since the new advisor is also closer in age to the G2s, George hopes his children will be more comfortable reaching out to him versus their parents' advisor. Institutional knowledge is preserved, but new knowledge is being developed to carry across to the next generation.

- The FTC's Education Committee, composed of G2 and the new Independent Director, chose the education programming focus to meet their needs.

- Because the FTC is not currently overseeing any charitable trusts, the family decided to use the Philanthropy Committee as a formalized forum for discussions on how to align family philanthropic ideas so that they can identify potential areas of family charitable involvement. The committee, comprised of only family members, gathers after each FTC Board meeting.

- George took a unique approach to the formation of the Family Business Asset Committee. He isn't ready to place voting shares of the family business in an irrevocable trust until he and his wife have passed, so the composition of the Family Business Asset Committee is cross-referenced in the FTC's governing documents and his revocable estate plan. This allows George to balance his desire to maintain exclusive control during his lifetime and name the mem-

FTC Structures: Case Studies

bers of the Family Business Asset Committee, ensuring a seamless transition of governance for the family business at the right time.

- The FTC governing documents also contemplate spouses serving on the Board and FTC committees. After much deliberation, the FTC governing documents provide that spouses may serve on the FTC Board and committees after being married for 15 years to a lineal descendent. This requirement aligns with the family's value of emphasizing the importance of long-term commitment to family involvement.

This case demonstrates how an FTC can serve the family well today by enhancing family cohesion and education while also establishing a seamless governance transition across generations.

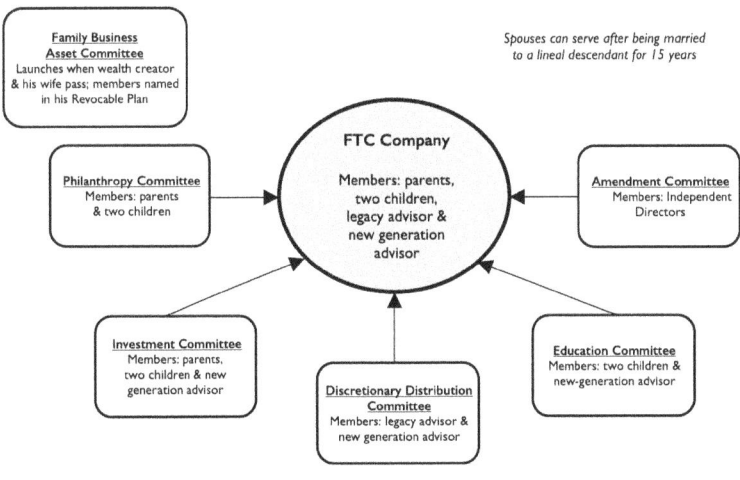

Case Study #5
Privacy & Confidentiality is Important—Together yet Separate

Motivation for Setting up the FTC: Trustee Succession and Family Business Shareholder Decisions

With over 50 legacy trusts, the Moreau family faced trustee succession challenges, especially because the rising generation showed reluctance to take on this important responsibility in the future. They had tried using a corporate bank trustee for a few trusts. However, it hadn't been a positive experience because of frustrations with getting information, as well as the corporate trustee's reluctance to hold concentrated family business assets. Simultaneously, they sought to solidify the family's control over the family business and its trajectory from a shareholder perspective.

The family's unique privacy and confidentiality preferences led to the establishment of a separate Investment Committee and Discretionary Distribution Committee for each family branch. While this structure may appear administratively complex, it catered to the Moreau's specific family structure. For example, the Investment Committees facilitated private discussions and decision-making around reinvesting in the family business.

With their privacy preserved, the FTC functioned as an effective vehicle for harmonizing the family's business interests while maintaining confidentiality. The Board, comprising representatives from each family branch and two Independent Directors, provided trust administration oversight without interfering in the private decisions of the Investment and Discretionary Distribution Committees. This approach allowed the family to manage their wealth and business with both unity and autonomy.

For the Moreau family, this case exemplifies how an FTC can be intricately tailored to meet the unique needs and preferences of a family, even when they prioritize both togetherness and confidentiality.

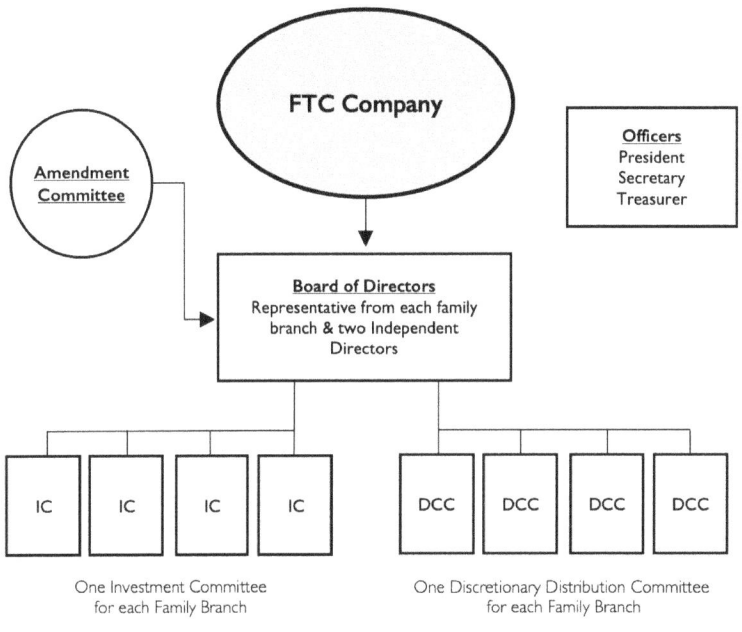

CHAPTER 7

Ongoing Operations

ESTABLISHING AND OPERATING an FTC is a multifaceted effort that extends beyond the mere creation of a legal entity. There are operational considerations, too, given the FTC is a fiduciary. It is responsible for the effective management of family assets and the mitigation of potential risks. Let's look more closely at some operational considerations.

Document, Document, Document!

The number one rule to follow when running an FTC is the mantra "document, document, document." Maintaining complete and accurate records of decision making and actions taken by the FTC through its board and committees is vital when providing fiduciary services. These records serve a dual purpose. First, they form the historical record of an FTC becoming the record of its fiduciary responsibility and compliance with statutory obligations and best practices. Second, they constitute an effective shield against potential challenges by beneficiaries in the future, providing tangible evidence of a well-considered decision-making process. This practice isn't just advisable; it's imperative.

Even if Unlicensed, Act "As If" Licensed for Protection

An FTC, whether licensed or unlicensed, should function as if it were licensed, where appropriate. This preemptive approach, though not legally mandated, provides the FTC with a layer of fiduciary protection that extends across multiple dimensions. By adhering to the standards and best practices typically expected of licensed entities, even when not compelled to do so by statute, the FTC safeguards the interests of both existing and future beneficiaries, including those yet to be born—plus directors, officers and committee members. It strengthens the FTC's operational framework from potential litigation challenges.

Prepare and Follow a Policy and Procedure Manual

The core operational document of a well-run FTC lies in the careful development and adherence to a detailed Policy and Procedure Manual (PPM). Th PPM delineates the comprehensive procedures guiding the FTC's operations and frequently it guides the documentation process through the use of convenient worksheets developed to document the well-reasoned decision making. This document helps the FTC's leadership to thoughtfully navigate through numerous decisions. The worksheets can be developed to walk decision-makers through important points of consideration when making decisions from onboarding a trust to making a discretionary distribution to investment processes. Its role is not confined to a static set of rules; rather, it can adapt to the needs as the FTC expands over time and be amended by the Board.

More Accountability through Formalization

Accountability and transparency are established in an FTC through formalized processes. Meetings, conducted regularly and systematically, form the hub of this process. The meeting minutes capture decisions and strategic insights. An annual review and update of each trust ensures investments are being regularly monitored and the FTC has current information on the beneficiaries for informed decision making. Having knowledge of any changes in the beneficiary's life is an important part of decision-making—particularly for distributions. This dedication to formality ensures that the FTC continues to operate in the best interests of the beneficiaries, and thus, the family.

Regular Board Meetings

Regular Board meetings are essential for the proper functioning of FTC governance. For example, Ohio requires a minimum of two meetings a year—one with a quorum of the Board physically present in Ohio. These meetings, conducted according to structured agendas, serve as the forum where important strategic and compliance decisions are made. And they underscore the importance of continuous communication and strategic planning within the FTC's operational landscape.

Consider an Agreed-Upon Procedure Audit

Beyond the realm of statutory mandates, an FTC, whether licensed or not, may consider having an agreed-upon procedure audit done

Ongoing Operations

by an outside expert. This audit, conducted by independent professionals, offers an external lens through which the FTC's operations are scrutinized. Its significance lies not only in bolstering operational efficiencies but also in signaling the FTC's steady commitment to best practices and operational excellence.

CHAPTER 8

Parting Thoughts: Thinking of an FTC as a Solution

Throughout this book, I have highlighted and demonstrated various motivators for families to set up an FTC. For a succinct summary, below are the four key concerns faced by multigenerational families that should prompt a family to become educated about how an FTC can be a solution in their wealth strategy.

Solution #1: Trustee Succession

Multigenerational estate planning can be complex and involve many players, and the role of the trustee is key. Trustees are responsible for managing and administering trust assets for the benefit of family members. For multigenerational planning, who will be the current trustee, but also the future trustee.

Here are some of the key advantages of an FTC when considering trustee succession:

Developing a Permanent Trustee Solution—One of the fundamental advantages offered by FTCs is their ability to develop a permanent trustee solution. This is achieved by establishing a corporation or limited liability company to serve as the trustee. Unlike individual trustees whose roles may change due to life events or unforeseen circumstances, the FTC remains a steadfast entity, ensuring that trust management remains uninterrupted. This permanence is invaluable, providing a reliable foundation for the family's wealth management strategies and reinforcing their commitment to preserving their legacy.

Standardizing Trustee Succession—Trustee succession can be a source of confusion and potential conflicts within families, particularly when different branches or generations have selected different trustees. FTCs address this issue head-on because the FTC *is* the trustee. This allows families to standardize their trustee succession plans across the whole family.

Opportunities for Asset Maintenance—Maintaining closely held assets or exploring alternative investment options are family goals easily managed by an FTC. An FTC provides families with the flexibility to continue managing assets that hold legacy or strategic value to the family—even if it's a concentrated asset in the trust. It also offers opportunities to explore alternative investments that align with evolving financial goals and market conditions.

Sustaining the Family Legacy—At the heart of trustee succession within an FTC is the objective of sustaining the family legacy over multiple generations. Through the required family ownership and control of an FTC, it enables families to pass on not only their wealth but also their values, traditions, and heritage to future generations.

Transitioning from Individual Fiduciary Liability—An essential legal aspect of trusteeship is the transition from individual fiduciary liability for individual trustees (often family members) to benefiting from the "business judgment" rule under an FTC. Individual family members serving as trustees move from bearing personal liability when making decisions in their capacity as trustees to enjoying the additional fiduciary protection afforded by following formal policies and procedures bolstered by proper documentation.

Solution #2: Control of the Family Wealth Strategy

Forming an FTC offers families a crucial advantage—maintaining control over their family wealth—whether liquid or a family business. For family businesses, shareholder decisions for shares transitioned to trusts can be made by family members ensuring the family's vision and legacy continue. This balance is achieved through a flexible structure allowing family involvement at the FTC Board and Committee levels—such as family members participating on the Family Business Asset Committee.

In practical terms, families often prefer concentrating shareholder decisions within a smaller group of family members and trusted advisors with the necessary expertise. For instance, the decision to elect the Board of Directors for the operating entity is critical. An FTC can establish a Family Business Asset Committee and another overseeing liquid asset investments, each requiring distinct expertise. Clearly defined job descriptions for FTC positions spell out required experience and essential characteristics, promoting family harmony by setting clear expectations for various family member roles.

Solution #3: Family Governance

One of the many advantages of an FTC is the ability for a family to keep family members engaged in the family enterprise beyond working in the family business. For those not interested in family business opportunities, involvement in the FTC—on its board and committees—may be of interest.

FTC boards are frequently comprised of Family Branch Directors who are given the opportunity to demonstrate their leadership skills. In addition, two optional committees for an FTC—an Education Committee and a Family Engagement Committee—can help, respectfully, educate family members as well as plan "family glue" activities to keep the family connecting beyond a shareholder meeting format. With this broader breadth of opportunities, more family members may find an opportunity of interest that matches their skills to provide them a platform to engage and "shine" within the family enterprise.

Solution #4: Enhancing the Trustee-Beneficiary Relationship

Navigating the complex dynamics of grantor/trustee/beneficiary relationships can pose significant challenges due to varying objectives in each role. Strengthening these connections and ensuring transparency regarding trust terms and decision-making processes is essential for fostering positive trustee/beneficiary interactions. When different family trusts have separate trustees overseeing them, beneficiaries often receive disparate, and at times conflicting, information. This can lead to confusion and erode trust among family members. Typically, family members engage in discussions and information-sharing to compensate for this lack of clarity. An FTC can be structured to encourage open communication, provide educational opportunities, and even facilitate mentorship among these relationships, ultimately fostering greater trust within the family and the family business.

Who Sets Up FTCs?

Families that create an FTC often share a common set of characteristics and objectives. Here is a list of the most common reasons why families use FTCs.

- Families having the goal of keeping the economic benefit of the family legacy for family members

- Families doing multigenerational estate planning and taking advantage of the window of opportunity with the highest gift and estate tax exemption ever

- Families concerned about trustee succession and adapting to family changes over time

- Families wanting to keep family members "engaged" outside of the family business

- Families interested in educational opportunities—particularly for the rising generation

- Families wanting to infuse their mission, vision and values through a flexible governance structure tailored for the family

- Families at a transitional point in passing family wealth and/or a family business asset to future generations
- Families looking to maintain shareholder control over family business assets and related decisions
- Families interested in keeping the family cohesive and working together for generations
- Families with a family-owned business, real estate holdings, or partnership interests held in trusts
- Families desiring privacy and confidentiality
- Families striving to concentrate oversight of the family assets
- Families currently having trusted advisors in place, but looking to establish structure and cohesiveness to bring them together
- Families seeking liability protection for decision makers
- Families looking to better manage trustee fees and administrative costs

The Enduring Value of FTCs in Family Wealth Management

In an era marked by increasing complexity and evolving family dynamics, FTCs can be a beacon of stability and a tailored solution managing a family's wealth strategy. Its role can encompass a holistic approach that integrates family values, legacy preservation, philanthropy, and education into the fabric of wealth management.

FTCs offer families the unique opportunity to exercise control over their financial destinies, ensuring that wealth is not an end in itself but a means to achieve a higher purpose aligned with the family's core principles. These entities empower families to navigate the complexities of multigenerational wealth management with confidence and clarity.

As the custodians of family legacies, FTCs can play a pivotal role in preserving the heritage and values that define each family. Their flexibility, intended transparency, and commitment to customized solutions can serve a family well in the journey towards enduring multigenerational wealth and a lasting legacy.

Appendix

Countdown to 2026

Today Isn't Too Soon to Plan for Future Estate Tax Law Changes

By Gina G. Gurganus, CFP®, Clearstead

"To not decide is to decide"
—Harvey Cox

The topic of wealth transfer and legacy planning is often discussed with individuals and families who have accumulated wealth; however, it's a discussion that typically spans years, if not decades. When considering how to pass wealth to the next generation, the options may seem endless: annual exclusion gifts, direct transfers, Roth conversions, irrevocable trusts, and intra-family lending to name a few. This, paired with the complexity that comes with legacy planning decisions, may leave many families with incomplete estate plans or plans that don't fully take advantage of the current estate tax law and the window of opportunity it presents.

What is the current estate tax law? The 2017 Tax Cuts and Jobs Act (TCJA) nearly doubled the lifetime estate and gift tax exemption ("lifetime exemption") from $5.6 million for individuals and $11.18 million for married couples, to $11.18 million and $22.36 million, respectively. For 2024, the inflation adjusted lifetime exemption is $12.92 million per person and $25.84 million for a married couple. This means an individual can "remove" $12.92 million from their estate, allowing these assets to pass estate tax free if the proper planning is put in place. Under current law, this increased lifetime exemption is scheduled to sunset, or revert, back to 2017 levels (adjusted for inflation) at the end of 2025.

What could this mean for you and your family? If TCJA sunsets as planned, the estate and gift exemption could be reduced to approximately $7 million per individual and $14 million for a married couple, depending on inflation over the next few years. This change could create a taxable estate for many individuals and families who currently would pass assets to the next generation free of estate tax. Currently, the maximum estate tax rate is 40 percent on taxable amounts greater than $1 million above the exemption amount. Therefore, an estate above the lifetime exemption amount would be reduced by the 40-percent tax before passing assets to your family members. Let's look at a few different scenarios to illustrate this on the following graphs.

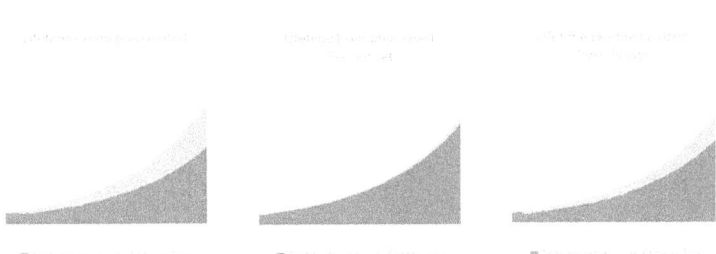

How do you lock in your exemption now? Trusts are one of the most popular and effective ways to remove assets from your estate. When properly drafted, trusts can significantly reduce your estate that is subject to the 40-percent estate tax rate or even eliminate the estate tax burden altogether. There are various types of trusts to consider when examining how to utilize your lifetime exemption depending on your unique financial situation. Even the appreciation of the assets placed in certain trusts would not be subject to estate taxes, thus "freezing" those assets out of your estate as well. Below are some specific examples of trusts used for this purpose.

A Dynasty Trust is drafted with the intention of passing assets from one generation to another in perpetuity without incurring estate taxes. To accomplish this, a dynasty trust may be funded up to the current lifetime exemption ($26.88 million, as discussed above), which removes these assets and the future appreciation from your taxable estate thus avoiding the 40-percent estate tax. To be effective, the trust must be irrevocable, and the grantors (donors) must give up "dominion and control" of the assets. Assets in a dynasty trust are managed by a trustee designated by the grantor for the benefit of beneficiaries (typically the grantors' descendants). The trustee is responsible for managing the assets in the trust according to the terms of the trust. Given the multigenerational duration that is characteristic of a dynasty trust, significant thought and consideration should be given to the trust terms and individuals named in various roles in the trust.

A Spousal Lifetime Access Trust ("SLAT") is a type of Dynasty Trust. A SLAT is an irrevocable trust where the grantor makes a gift to a trust for the benefit of his or her spouse (and potentially children or other family members) to utilize the lifetime exemption. The spouse that is the primary beneficiary of the trust may request distributions, if needed, during his or her lifetime.

Considerations for Family Business Interests

Will your estate have the liquidity to pay the estate tax liability? For many business owners, much of their wealth is tied up in the family business. With federal estate tax generally due nine months following the date of death, planning for liquidity to pay the estate taxes can be imperative to avoid unattractive options such as the need to liquidate the family business to meet the estate tax obligation. It is important for family-business owners to start planning today for the shareholder transition of their business while the lifetime exemption is at an all-time high. Additionally, it can be advantageous to remove these assets from the estate before significant appreciation of a family business occurs.

What steps can you take now to prepare? Start planning your legacy today. As 2026 draws closer, we encourage you to engage your financial planner to start the discussion around utilizing your lifetime exemption ahead of the scheduled sunset. As time goes on, many financial planners and attorneys may find it increasingly difficult to accommodate all clients and the advanced estate planning required to utilize the lifetime exemption prior to the sunset.

As a business owner, giving up "dominion and control" of ownership of the family business by putting the ownership in a trust may give you pause. That's where an FTC comes in. It is a powerful planning technique that may be a solution for a wide range of family-business owners.

Endnotes

1. Goldstone, H.; Hughes, J.E.; Whitaker, K. *Family Trusts: A Guide for Beneficiaries, Trustees, Trust Protectors, and Trust Creators* (Bloomberg), 2015.

2. smartasset.com/financial-advisor/the-great-wealth-transfer/

3. Perdue, M. *How to Make Your Family Business Last* (R.J. Myers), 2017.

4. Family Business Alliance., Conway Center for Family Business

5. Zellweger, T.M; Nason, R.S; Nordqvist, M. *"From Longevity of Firms to Transgenerational Entrepreneurship of Families: Introducing Family Entrepreneurial Orientation." Family Business Review*, Vol 25, Issue 2, 2012.

6. familybusinesscenter.com/resources/family-business-facts/

7. Seaman, R.N. *A Vibrant Vision: The Entrepreneurship of Multigenerational Family Business* (Seaman Corp.), 2019.

8. Williams, R; Preisser, V. *Preparing Heirs (Robert D. Reed)*, 2014.

9. Kachaner, N; Stalk, G; Bloch, A. *"What You Can Learn From Family Business." Harvard Business Review*, 2012.

10. Allegretti, C. *Global Family Business Survey* (Deloitte Development LLC.), 2019.

11. middlemarketcenter.org/Media/Documents/preparing-for-major-business-transition-in-middle-market-companies.pdf

12. massmutual.com/business/business-owners/

13. Astrachan, J.H.; Shanker, M.C. "Family Businesses' Contribution to the U.S. Economy: A Closer Look." *Family Business Review*, 2003.

14. Schervish, R. *Wealth with Responsibility: Study 2000* (Bankers Trust Private Banking/Deutsche Bank Group), 1999.

15. Allegretti, C.

16. The Ohio Family Trust Company Act was passed in 2016 and became effective in September 2016. As many states offering private trust company statutes are western states, many advisors in Ohio were unfamiliar with the benefits of setting up a Family Trust Company. It's important to work with an advisor familiar with the set up and operation of Family Trust Companies in Ohio.

17. psychologytoday.com/us/blog/the-stories-of-our-lives/202303/family-stories-are-the-ties-that-bind-us/

www.ingramcontent.com/pod-product-compliance
Lightning Source LLC
Chambersburg PA
CBHW051620010526
44119CB00009B/219